The five
feel-good factors

By the same author
Natural Pain Relief
Peaceful Sleep

JAN SADLER

The five feel-good factors

The key to true happiness

Index by Ann Griffiths

SAFFRON WALDEN
THE C.W. DANIEL COMPANY LIMITED

First published in Great Britain in 2001.
by The C.W. Daniel Company Limited
1 Church Path, Saffron Walden,
Essex, CB10 1JP, United Kingdom

ISBN 0 85207 345 3

Designed by Jane Humphrey
Produced in association with Book Production Consultants plc,
25–27 High Street, Chesterton, Cambridge, CB4 1ND
Typeset by Cambridge Photosetting Services
Printed and bound by Hillman Printers (Frome) Ltd, England

Introduction   1

section 1 – Free your inner powers   5

1. Listen to Your Inner Voice   7
2. Making Time for Yourself   10
3. The Bodymind Network   11
4. How to Interact with the Bodymind Network   12
5. Evidence for the Bodymind Network   13
6. Introducing the Bodymind Directions   14
7. The Start-up Bodymind Directions   16
8. The Tuning-in Session and the Start-up Bodymind
   Directions   18
9. Making Your Own Bodymind Directions   21
10. Fast Track Communication System   23
11. Establishing the 'Yes' and 'No' Signals   24
12. Receiving Answers to Your Questions   29
13. The Higher Level Communication System   30
14. The Higher Level Communication System Relaxation
    Session   32
15. The Inner Power of Visualisation   36
16. 'The Key to True Happiness' Visualisation   38
17. Unleash Your Inner Powers NOW!   42
18. Review   42

section 2 – Find inner peace   45

1. Find Inner Peace   47
2. Your Body Speaks For You   48
3. 'Breathe and Smile' Mantra   51
4. Other Opportunities for the 'Breathe and Smile'
   Mantra   53
5. Body Smiling   55
6. Maximise Your Inner Peace and Happiness   57
7. Just Being   59
8. The Benefits of 'Just Being'   61
9. A Simple Meditation Exercise   63
10. Meditation for Inner Peace   65
11. Mantra Meditation   68

12. Sharing Your Inner Peace   70

13. Inner Peace and Your Relationships   71

14. Bodymind Directions for Inner Peace   78

15. Review   80

section 3 – Feel good about yourself 83

1. The Path to Feeling Good About Yourself   85

PART ONE – *Happy Thoughts Make a Happy Life*

2. Automatic Bodymind Directions   87

3. The Power in Your Mind   89

4. Interpretation of Situations   91

5. Define Your Automatic Negative Bodymind
Directions/Thoughts   92

6. Catch Your Automatic Negative Bodymind
Directions   95

7. Challenging Your Automatic Negative Bodymind
Directions   98

8. Eliminating Your Automatic Negative Bodymind
Directions   99

9. What Governs Your Life?   102

PART TWO – *Feeling Good About Your Body*

10. Your Body Image   103

11. Keep Moving!   104

12. The Shake Dance   106

13. The Energy Dial   107

14. Breathing   109

15. Breathing Practice   110

16. Visualisation   111

17. Visualisation – 'Your Ideal You'   113

18. The Power of Bodymind Directions for
Feeling Good About Yourself   116

19. Review   119

section 4 – Follow your dreams 121

1. Your Purpose in Life   123

2. Seeking Your First Goal   124

3. Use Your Inner Wisdom to Find Your Goals   125

4. Choosing Your No. 1 Goal   127

5. The Success Route   128

6. Using Your Inner Powers for Goal Success   130

7. Preparing to Achieve Your Dream   132

8. Pushing the Walls of the 'Comfort Zone Bubble'   133

9. Taking the First Step   135

10. 'Total Fulfilment' Visualisation   135

11. Keeping on Track   142

12. Bodymind Directions for Achieving Your Goal   145

13. Review   146

section 5 – Fill your life with love   149

1. That Loving Feeling   151

2. More About Loving   152

3. Decide to be Loving   153

4. A Loving Meditation   155

5. How to Nurture that Loving Feeling   161

6. Visualisation with Your Inner Child   163

7. Healing Emotional Situations   165

8. Hugging and Loving Meditation   168

9. Loving, Giving and Receiving   170

10. Bodymind Directions for Loving   172

11. Review   174

Summary   175

Index   180

contents

Introduction

1 Free Your Inner Powers
2 Find Inner Peace
3 Feel Good About Yourself
4 Follow Your Dreams
5 Fill Your Life With Love

The Five Feel-good Factors are, indeed, the key to true happiness. To live in happiness and at peace with yourself and to live to your full potential is your very purpose in life. Most of us live our days unaware that we already have within us all we need to transform our lives. The ideas in this book will show you how to maximise your full happiness, success and health potential through each of the Feel-good Factors using the wonderful creative powers of your inner-most self.

No matter what your current circumstances, you now have the opportunity, as well as the ability, to lead a fulfilled and a happy life. Whatever age you are, whatever your present position in life, you can still find a little time and space to devote to yourself and discover how to achieve happiness in your life.

This isn't just a dream. You may imagine that many changes will need to be made, but all you need to do is to *decide* you want more peace, happiness and fulfilment in your life and with that one decision you will find things actually begin to move. You will become more open and aware, and receptive to positive ideas that will be for your greater good.

You need only make one or two small alterations at first and you will find that as you continue to grow and, as your attitude towards life is transformed, positive resources will be drawn towards you and then any changes that once seemed out of reach suddenly become easy. By your very interest in reading this book you have, as of now, taken your decision to be happy and consequently have already made that first vital change to your life.

With your decision to be happy, you have taken your first step on a new golden path through life. When you decide to be happy you will discover that, because the world is a mirror to your mind, happiness will gradually be reflected back to you more and more. When you decide to be happy you will see the world in a new joyful way. You will discover unknown delights and treasures that were previously hidden from you. You will find people respond to you in a different, more loving, positive and co-operative way, and situations that once seemed difficult now can be seen as being an opportunity or a new chance for you. You really can teach the world out there and the people in it to respond to you in the way you want. It is true to say that what you give out is reflected back in abundance.

Each Feel-good Factor has a section of its own which contains dynamic and easy to follow techniques that really work, allowing you to create a balanced life where you achieve true happiness and success in every area: your health, your leisure time, your career, your relationships and in your personal development and spiritual life.

Some of the inspiring and valuable ideas to help you to unlock your happiness potential are short and relatively simple, others require a little more time and thought. They vary from the practical to the imaginative, using new creative visualisation techniques. You may feel that some of the exercises are currently more relevant to you than others, if so, leave aside those for which you have no immediate need. You may return to them later if you wish.

The Five Feel-good Factors cover many aspects of your life. The first Feel-good Factor shows you exciting ways to develop your inner powers for a life of true happiness, peace of mind and fulfilment. Your Inner Wisdom has amazing, almost magical powers, including the ability to interact with the two-way pathway which exists between your body and your mind, the 'Bodymind Connection'. Your introduction to this new and original technique will empower you to make transforming changes to your body, mind and spirit.

The second and third Feel-good Factors describe wonderful ways to cultivate inner peace and to feel good about yourself. The fourth Feel-good Factor reveals to you your deepest dreams and desires and shows you how to achieve them quickly and easily. The final Feel-good Factor is all about the art of loving, and filling your life with harmony and balance, creating rich and joyful relationships with all who come into your world.

A final word about achieving happiness in adversity. At times, we all are faced with tough choices and challenging events, but even on these occasions, when you know how, you can still find a centre of acceptance, peace and comfort deep within yourself and know that you will overcome the challenges facing you, emerging stronger and happier for it. This knowledge is true happiness indeed.

You may already be conscious of the kind of life you want to live, you may even now be on your way towards that life, or you may still be unaware that it is possible to gain control of your life, making simple yet beneficial changes to the way you live. However far you are along the road, or whether you have yet to take the first steps of the exciting journey ahead of you, this book will guide and support you along the pathway to fulfilment and true happiness.

The book doesn't have to be read straight through. However, it's best if you read Feel-good Factor One first and then you can choose which of the following four Feel-good Factors you read next as they are self-contained units.

Free your inner powers

1. Listen to Your Inner Voice

Freeing your inner powers just has to be the first Feel-good Factor as it is one of the most enabling and enriching. With your inner powers liberated you can make wonderful changes in your whole life. Think how great it would be to take advice from the inner wisdom that resides within you and to have a positive input into your health to stimulate your body's natural healing processes into action. Best of all, think how terrific it would be to be able to make yourself feel happy and sparkling and full of vitality with just a few simple words to your inner self.

Everyone longs to be happy, but few know that it is possible to *decide* to be happy and, with the right strategies, cultivate happiness. Many people are **waiting** for happiness, waiting for it to arrive at some point in the future when they think they will then surely find happiness. However, happiness is not something that is to be waited for. Happiness is found here and now, in the present time, as you are *right now*. Yes, even with your current challenges and with any testing situations in which you find yourself, it is still possible to find happiness deep within yourself.

To feel happy and fulfilled basically you need to feel *good* about yourself and to accept yourself as the person that you are including whatever aspects of your personality or your life you may, at this moment, perceive as being undesirable. You feel happy and good about yourself when you take part in activities that involve you totally and with which you are comfortable, activities that give you peace of mind; activities that are enriching, totally absorbing and satisfying and are for your greater good, for the best and activities where you invest time, thought and energy in the well-being of others. A happy life is a balanced life, lively and vital, rich in experience, with time spent cherishing every area of your life, consciously focusing your attention on the joyful aspects within your world, where you treat yourself and others kindly and with compassion.

At the moment your path may be one where there is no time for your creative energies to blossom, where you are rushed, stressed or seemingly blocked in some other way by, perhaps, a work, relationship or health issue, swept along by events and other people's energies. Today there are so many distractions, so much information to deal with and so many responses to make that your time and energy is sure to be at a premium. Your days may be crammed with activities, tasks, commitments and duties, so that there never seems to be enough space to do anything with satisfaction and time to spare. Even your weekends, when you may be away from work itself, probably tend to be packed full with yet more activities and chores. This means you are likely to begin the next week as you finished the last, tired, harassed and over-stretched. Major 'life-events' and even small irritations may add to the stress, making you feel pressurised and unfulfilled.

If some of this sounds familiar territory to you, this is the time when you need to heed that small voice inside yourself that says 'This is not how I want to live my life'. We all receive these messages from time to time, and usually ignore them, but we all know deep inside ourselves when we are either 'on line' or 'off centre', 'on the path' or off it, in or out of accord with our greatest desires and needs. These messages or feelings of unease within yourself are telling you that you are not focusing on your real desires and needs, have become less true to your real self. *Listen to those messages!* They are the authentic voice of your Inner Wisdom, your greatest inner power, the part of you that is your Highest Self, a benevolent all-knowing intelligence that has access to your whole being; physical, emotional, mental and spiritual.

A happy life is one where your actions and thoughts stem from the deep wisdom of this higher inner self. Although often unused, we all have this natural inner sense of goodness and knowledge, this Inner Wisdom. When your life is guided by this inner power you will find you will always choose paths which are supporting and nourishing, paths which lead irrevocably to joy and happiness. Remember always that your life is yours to use as you will, in whatever way you choose. **You** are the one with the power, even if you have never or only rarely realised this.

The ability to connect and converse with this super-intelligence will enable you to make positive and profound changes in your life and the lives of those around you. Your Inner Wisdom always knows what is best for you and which choices are in your best interests to follow. This inner force can answer any question you care to ask it, whether about your career or your relationships and, if you listen with sensitivity, will always give you the answer that is in your true interest and that is for your greater good.

The power of your inner self is such that, with the correct commands to your Bodymind Network, you can use it to initiate and support your healing processes, often creating remarkable therapeutic results, energising and healing you, at emotional, mental, spiritual and physical levels. A simple technique is used to open up the communication pathways with your Inner Wisdom which allows you to use its wonderful powers to influence the two-way pathway that exists between your mind and your body, your Bodymind Connection. Each one, both your body and your mind, is capable of influencing the other to bring about desired alterations in your body, mind and spirit. This is a new and original technique which uses short, easy-to-follow Bodymind Directions which empower you to intercede with the Bodymind Connection and bring about the transformations you desire.

You may already know the kind of life you would like to lead, or you may even now be on your way towards that life. Your Inner Wisdom will support you in any changes you wish to make, allowing you to dissolve blockages that may be hindering you. You can tap into your extraordinary inner powers to create a balanced and rounded life with the emotions you want to feel, the health you want to enjoy and the happiness and successes you deserve.

A powerful relationship with your Inner Wisdom will enable you to lead your life as though guided by your own best friend, your own personal Life Trainer. Your Inner Wisdom is a force and a friend who is always truthful, always supportive, healing and empowering, and always available to you – when you know how to gain access to its energies. You will soon learn how to obtain fast and direct communication with your Inner Wisdom. You and your body and mind will be able to enjoy an interactive relationship in your full conscious control at any time, without the need of lengthy relaxation procedures. No matter how busy your day, you will soon discover how you can clear any blocks to your creativity and joy and bring your life into equilibrium.

So, accept the challenge of facing those messages or feelings that tell you you are 'off the path' and begin to live your *real* life. Learn how to contact your inner self and learn how to interact with your amazing Bodymind Network to regain your place on the path of happiness, health and success. First of all, though, discover how you can find time to make these wonderful changes.

2. Making Time for Yourself

Making time and space for yourself to nurture and support yourself needn't be seen as an insurmountable challenge. Everyone can find the odd few minutes it takes to read a page or so of the book or to use any of the dynamic techniques in this book. At first you may have to deliberately MAKE time for yourself and snatch the odd few minutes here and there. Very soon you will find that, as your attitude changes in subtle ways, time *does* become available for you. Your priorities will change as you see the benefits of taking life more calmly and investing moments within it with more meaning. You will find that you value your 'ME-time' and reap the rewards from investing in yourself. You will discover that it is more essential to spend five or ten extra minutes on nurturing yourself than on chasing some everyday task. I know we all have various commitments, some more onerous or time consuming than others, but we still have an element of choice in how we use our time. At the moment, you can easily find a spare few minutes to use a technique whilst waiting in a queue, holding the line on the telephone, or in the bathroom or waiting for the computer to fire up.

Later on you may find you need to reassign some tasks and adjust your busy schedule, perhaps even dropping some commitments altogether, as you adapt your lifestyle to be more in tune with walking the path of happiness. These changes will come gradually and with no great effort because you will *want* to make them.

So, concern yourself only with the present, you're doing just fine as you are, merely accept the few odd moments given to you as an opportunity to use some of the quick and deceptively simple techniques you are about to learn. Do this and you will find that each day becomes steadily more and more as you would like it to be.

Begin the process of spending time on yourself by determining to participate in positive, enjoyable activities. Concentrate on being optimistic and *enjoying* your successes. Remember, it's *your* choice, *you* choose where you place your attention and upon what you focus; and so choose to place your attention on interesting, absorbing pursuits and you will be outward-looking, inspire confidence in yourself, and stay fulfilled and happy.

3. The Bodymind Network

There is an amazing conjunction between your mind and your body, each one influencing how the other functions. In this process, chemical messengers are constantly passed from one area to another. Dr. Pert of the Georgetown University Medical Center in Washington has found that intelligent information is passed via molecules and receptors between all the major systems of your body. Information is passed in both directions, your body feeding your mind and your mind feeding your body – body and mind as one entity. For example, your gut is lined with an extra dense layer of cells which means that your emotions can be felt there – your 'gut feelings'. It is well known that what goes on in your mind directly affects the working of your gut. If you feel apprehensive or frightened you can feel 'sick with worry', if you feel angry your gut motility is increased and your stomach starts churning, when you calm down gut activity decreases and your abdominal area quietens.

You, however, can interact in the processes of this 'Bodymind Network' and so affect the outcome. Your brain and your body are integrally and intricately linked together in the Bodymind Network. Through intervening in the Bodymind Network by feeding your brain, or your body, with the right messages or instructions you can have an input into various basic areas of body function such as your heart rate, reducing tension or relieving pain and many more subtle effects whereby you can change the path of your health dramatically. Influencing the Bodymind Network works both ways, of course. By quietening the body you then find you quieten the mind, by stimulating the body, you enliven the mind. The power is yours to change the way you feel and the way your body functions so, by implication, influence and change both your health and your emotional state.

We all possess a unique ability to heal ourselves but few people have the knowledge or the techniques to tap into their inner powers and use them for their own good. Read on and find out how you can become one of these people by learning how to interact successfully with your Bodymind Network.

4. How to Interact with the Bodymind Network

When you first learn to make contact with your Bodymind Network, it's best to take a little time out from the noise and rush of your busy day. At the outset the intelligence inside you needs space and quietness to make itself heard in your consciousness. Later on, when you are more experienced, you will be able to make contact with your inner self almost instantaneously and virtually anywhere. However, at the beginning, you need to take a few minutes when you have time and space, preferably early on in the day, to 'go within' yourself with a brief formal process to ensure you make a sound connection with that intelligence.

Firstly, you are going to learn how to give instructions to enhance your general well being and to energise your entire system, your body, mind and spirit. With these instructions you will find you can transform your mood in an instance. For example, instruct your Bodymind Network to make you feel calm and you will feel calm. Instruct your Bodymind Network to make you feel happy and you will feel happy. By having immediate physical evidence of the positive effects gained from these instructions you will be convinced of the power of your Bodymind Network, gain confidence in the process and learn to trust the responses from your inner self. Think of the immense satisfaction you will gain in discovering this power that is within you.

Secondly, you are going to learn to initiate and develop a wonderful question and answer system which will allow you to take full advantage of the deep knowledge of your higher intuitive self, which knows the answer to all your questions and quandaries. You can make simple enquiries about daily activities, such as if it would be good for you to eat another helping at mealtime, or you can ask more profound questions, such as if it is in your spiritual interest to take a particular course of action.

The response to your questions will come initially via the Bodymind Network which you will programme to give you simple 'yes' or 'no' answers. You can then learn a more advanced communication system which will use the full powers of your intuitive inner self to give more detailed answers.

Firstly, carry out the following experiment to prove to yourself the existence and the power of the Bodymind Network – it's simple and it's fun. Amaze yourself!

5. Evidence for the Bodymind Network

This test will show you that your Bodymind Network does exist and how you really can intervene in the process to influence how your body functions. In this experiment you will give instructions to your Bodymind Network which will show how your mind and body work together, without you yourself having any conscious input into the process.

Don't just read about it, this experiment really does need to be experienced for you to see the dramatic effect your words can have on your body, so take a few quiet moments to carry out this startling test.

1. For this experiment you will need a long, newish pencil. Use your less dominant hand, that is, the hand you don't write with, to hold the top of the pencil very firmly up in front of you between your index finger and your thumb. Now, place the index finger of the hand you write with on the pointed end of the pencil.

2. First of all, test the strength of your grip by trying to press down the pencil which you are holding very firmly between your index finger and your thumb. You will find this very difficult to do.

3. Now, hold the pencil as before and, just for the sake of this experiment, consciously introduce a negative instruction to your Bodymind Network,

'Finger and thumb get weaker and weaker, weaker and weaker.'

4. Repeat these words a few times and then try once more to press down the pencil with your other index finger. You will find the pencil is knocked down very easily indeed. Your muscles responded to your statement even though you yourself consciously did nothing at all.

5. Next, grip the pencil again with your index finger and thumb and this time introduce a positive instruction to your Bodymind Network,

'Finger and thumb get stronger and stronger, stronger and stronger.'

6. Repeat this instruction a few times and then try again to press down the pencil. You will find this time that your muscles are full of strength and power and the pencil cannot be easily knocked down. The positive instruction to your Bodymind Network gave instant strength to your finger and thumb.

This experiment will have given you some idea of the fantastic power of your Bodymind Network. Just think how great this is! Imagine the ways in which you can use this power! Think of the wonderful changes you can bring about, both instantly and long-term, with the right instructions. You really can have a major and positive input into how you feel, how your body functions and into improving your health and even your spiritual development.

6. Introducing the Bodymind Directions

You may be aware of the technique of saying affirmations to yourself in an attempt to induce a change in mood. Affirmations, however, can fail to imprint themselves convincingly in your mind. For example, if you say, *'I feel calm and confident'* when you are actually feeling the direct opposite you are giving contradictory messages to yourself. Inside yourself you know perfectly well you are *not* feeling calm and confident and so may not fully accept the affirmation thus passing inadequate messages on to the Bodymind Network. To overcome this, you can speak directly to your Bodymind Network instructing it to feel the way you want to feel.

The Bodymind Network works in a very direct, simple and straightforward way, therefore you need to make sure your instructions and questions are given with as much clarity as possible so there is no chance of being misunderstood. The instructions you use need to be easily assimilated and so they should be short, concise and, indeed, concentrated to their very essence, so their intention cannot be misinterpreted. They need to describe exactly what it is you want. So instead of saying, '*I feel calm and confident*', you *order* your Bodymind Network, '*Be calm and confident*'. This dictatorial approach can produce impressive results. Your Bodymind Network knows exactly what it is you want when it is stated so assertively – you demand and it obeys your demands and will produce the result you desire.

It is also most important that the commands are expressed in the positive. For example, if your desire is to feel calm and confident, give your instruction as '*Be calm and confident*' **not** '*Do not feel worried*'. If you express your wish in the negative, intelligent as your Bodymind Network is, it is still possible it could home in on the words 'feel worried', ignoring the two insignificant words 'do not' – with the unwanted result of feelings of anxiety being experienced. So, make sure that you always give your instructions stating what it is you actually want to achieve, in this case, to feel calm and confident.

Another very important point is to remember that you are giving the Bodymind Directions *to* yourself, instructing or ordering yourself to move towards a particular course of action, which is why it's best to construct your sentences to comply with this. For example, instead of saying, 'My health improves every day', you instruct or direct yourself by saying, 'Your health improves every day'. Try it out and see the distinction.

I call the instructions you give to your Bodymind Network 'the Bodymind *Directions*' because they point your Bodymind Network in the *direction* in which you want it to move.

Your inner self knows what is needed and what is good for you, so it is often more productive to direct, '*Generate whatever is necessary to cope with this situation*'. Your Bodymind Network will then produce the feeling that is most helpful to you at that moment in time. Your Inner Wisdom knows better than *you*, so when you say '*Generate whatever is necessary ....*' it will produce what you truly need, which is not necessarily what you *think* is needed to produce the desired result. Almost anything you ask for will be given to you or initiated. When you ask, your Bodymind Network will always respond in a way that is the best for you, sometimes with surprising and unexpected results.

For even more productive results formulate your Bodymind Directions in a progressive manner. For example, *'Feel calmer day by day'* or *'Feel more and more confident every day'*. You may find that instructions formulated in this way are more readily accepted by your Bodymind Network. The reason is that if you have been feeling, say, worried and stressed for a long time, this progressive way of stating what you want may be easier for your inner self to accommodate.

Read on now for more exciting information about how to give Bodymind Directions.

7. The Start-up Bodymind Directions

When you first use the power of your Bodymind Network to effect changes in your body, mind, emotions or spirit, it is best to start by giving the five 'Start-up Bodymind Directions'. Giving the Start-up Bodymind Directions will ensure you really have a strong contact with your body and your inner self so that you can begin to feel its power coursing through you. Later on, when you are more experienced, you can, if you wish, omit this stage and go straight to giving your own Directions to create whatever effect you want in your being and your life. However, if you find your own personal Directions aren't working as well as you had hoped, re-introduce these initial Start-up Bodymind Directions to re-charge and empower your system before giving your own individual Bodymind Directions.

What You May Experience

There is a variety of feelings you may experience when you give the Start-up Bodymind Directions. They may be physical and/or emotional. You will most likely experience slight feelings of energy moving through your body and a lightening of your mood creating an uplifting effect. However, you may not notice much reaction to the Directions at all, which is fine. Conversely, you may have a strong response with very noticeable energy shifts in your body or mood. Even if you aren't aware of very much initially, please don't assume that just because you don't feel anything that nothing *is* happening. Many positive shifts can be made at a very subtle level below your current level of perception without you necessarily being aware of them. Whatever you encounter, be assured it is only in your best interests and for your own good. This inner power always knows what is best for you and, because it is a force purely for good, it will allow only you to experience what you can accept and be comfortable with. So, be patient, and just continue to nurture and deepen your awareness of yourself. Please don't dismiss the method or tell yourself, 'It's not enough' if you notice only tiny changes. If you have been unaware of your body's nuances of feelings for a long time, you cannot expect a major transformation overnight. Nurse and nurture these new beginnings as though they were tiny seedlings which need your constant care and attention.

The first Start-up Bodymind Direction is designed to bring you calmness and confidence. The second will encourage a gentle smile and feelings of happiness and peace. The third will show you are willing to let go of negative patterns in your body, mind and spirit. The fourth will spread a warm and loving feeling inwardly to yourself and outwardly to others and the fifth will allow you to end on a really high note by encouraging extra feelings of great happiness and pleasure.

After giving the Start-up Bodymind Directions you will be ready to either carry on and go about your day with your batteries recharged, or ready to use any personal Bodymind Directions of your own. These personal Bodymind Directions would be relevant to your own needs at that time, perhaps health, career or emotional matters or something deeper such as a spiritual issue.

Controlling Your Responses

During the process of giving your Bodymind Directions you may wish either to increase or decrease your responses. It is perfectly possible to adjust any response so that it can be felt either more or less fully just by instructing your Bodymind Network with the appropriate phrase. The following are the type of phrases which will help to increase or slow down your reactions.

'More and more.'
'Faster than that.'
'Calmer and calmer.'
'Happier and happier.'
'Smile more and more.'

'Calmer and calmer every day.'

'Slower than this.'

'Not so fast.'

You can, of course, make up or adjust the phrases to suit your own particular needs.

Cancelling a Bodymind Direction

Always give 'clean', clear and precise Bodymind Directions. If you make an error in giving your Bodymind Directions, rather than stumble on which may cause confusion, it is far better to stop and begin again. So, if you make a mistake, just say, 'Cancel that' or 'Stop there' and then repeat your Bodymind Directions from the beginning of the sentence.

Now you have the basic background information, you are ready to learn how to begin giving the Start-up Bodymind Directions. Study the instructions carefully and be ready for some wonderful happenings.

8. The Tuning-in Session and the Start-up Bodymind Directions

Before You Begin

Before you give the Start-up Bodymind Directions you need to commence the whole process by quietening your body and mind, thus making it more receptive and ready to receive your instructions.

Take your time when you come to giving the Start-up Directions, they must not be hurried or rushed through. Leave a pause between each Start-up Bodymind Direction of at least half a minute; however, take just as long as you like. Remember, you may not notice anything dramatic happening, as any responses are likely to be subtle. The pause will give time, firstly, for the Start-up Bodymind Direction to be accepted and understood by your inner self so that it can initiate the process you are asking for and, secondly, time for you to feel the method begin to work in your body and mind. You really do have to allow sufficient quiet time for this to happen. Keep an open mind and don't *expect* anything in particular to happen. Pay attention to yourself and just *notice* what is happening. Remember you can intensify any response by saying, 'more and more' or 'faster than this', or similar phrases of your own as appropriate.

Although it doesn't take very long, please don't rush any part of the process. You are not trying to 'get anywhere', you are just 'being'. This 'non-endgaining' approach is most important.

FIRST STEP / *Tuning-in To Your Body*

Find a quiet place where you can be undisturbed for about ten minutes.

Stand with your feet about a foot apart. Look directly ahead, or very slightly down.

Still your body and mind by saying quietly to yourself, 'STOP', and stop what you are doing.

STAND STILL – and WAIT. Allow yourself to relax. Don't fidget or shift from one foot to the other, don't do *anything* except become aware of your body. This hiatus, or short period where you are doing nothing, will give your body and mind time to settle and come into the present.

Stand like this for one or two minutes, without **doing** anything. As you stand there, just become more and more aware of your body. With this increased awareness, you may become conscious of impressions of tightness in parts of your body, perhaps around your lower back, legs or armpits. Don't try to alter anything, just carry on noticing what is taking place. You may observe after a while that any tense sensations in your arms and legs begin to ease and you may have the impression that your back has altered slightly, straightened and come into balance. You may also feel other parts of your body move and change position a little. If your body wants to move, allow it to do so by itself without interfering in any way. If you do notice any movements or energy shifts, just let them happen and welcome the changes as beneficial. As your attention and awareness grow in sensitivity you will begin to notice ever more subtle changes and movements.

1

After a minute or two, when your body and mind have quietened, and when it feels right to you, begin the second step.

SECOND STEP / *Give the Start-up Bodymind Directions*

When your body and mind have stilled at the end of the Tune-in, give the following Start-up Bodymind Directions. Say them out aloud or just under your breath with a clear, gentle but firm voice, as though speaking to a small child.

1. **Feel calm and confident.**
(PAUSE AND WAIT, NOTICE ANY RESPONSE)

2. **Smile and feel happy.**
(PAUSE AND WAIT, NOTICE ANY RESPONSE)

3. **Release anything negative from your body, mind and spirit.**
(PAUSE AND WAIT, NOTICE ANY RESPONSE)

4. **Fill your entire being with loving kindness towards yourself and the world.**
(PAUSE AND WAIT, NOTICE ANY RESPONSE)

5. **Feel full of vibrant health and energy. Sparkle with confidence. Glow with joy.**
(PAUSE AND WAIT, NOTICE ANY RESPONSE)

Remember: When you are new to these ideas you may not notice at first very much at all. This is fine. Don't assume that because you haven't noticed anything it means that nothing has taken place, this is not necessarily true. With patience, attention and mindfulness, increased awareness will come.

THIRD STEP / *Review*

It is best not to end the Start-up Bodymind Directions by rushing straight off to whatever activity you want to return to or begin.

Instead, take a few minutes more to feel and **ENJOY** the peace and any other sensations you have created. Remember, these feelings are **yours.** They are within you always and only await the opportunity to be reawakened by you once more.

Using the Start-up Bodymind Directions

Use the Tune-in session and give the full Start-up Bodymind Directions at least twice a day, for this you need only spend ten minutes or so at a time. This practice will ensure you gain confidence in the effectiveness of your interaction with the Bodymind Network and will also allow you to become closer and closer to your inner self. You will become more and more comfortable in communicating with your inner self and achieve increasingly effective responses when giving your Bodymind Directions.

Once you are experienced and practised you can use the Start-up Bodymind Directions as and when you need them for instant effect. For instance, you may need to call for support in a stressful situation; then you can just 'drop down inside yourself' and quietly instruct yourself (out aloud, or inside your head, if necessary), *'Be calm and confident'* and then pause to allow the effect to be felt in your body.

In the other sections of the book you will find examples of Bodymind Directions relevant to the subjects in that section.

When you have opened up your Bodymind Network with the Tune-in session and become calmer and more receptive with the Start-up Bodymind Directions you can begin to work on any issues that are in the forefront of your mind.

Read on for Bodymind Direction suggestions for promoting and strengthening links with your inner self for inner calm, emotional and spiritual balance and for your happiness.

9. Making Your Own Bodymind Directions

Instructions for Bodymind Directions

Your Bodymind Directions should always be formulated with happiness in mind, whether the Directions are for yourself or whether they include other people. Use your Bodymind Directions only for good, with the aim of spreading love and fulfilment to all, whatever their situation or whatever you perceive they have done to you.

If your Bodymind Directions involve thoughts of retribution, vengeance or redress against someone or something, these negative aspirations will surely rebound upon you because you will attract people and situations into your life with similar negative qualities. There is an old law of attraction which brings you into contact with people and situations of the same frame of mind as yourself. To work with this law and benefit from it, when you construct your Bodymind Directions incorporate happiness and you will draw happiness towards you. Let your purpose be to draw happiness, good and contentment towards you both for yourself and for those who come into contact with you. In this way you will fulfil your real purpose in life – to live a life of happiness, peace and well being.

Summary of Instructions for Bodymind Directions

Always compose your Bodymind Directions with the following points in mind:

Bodymind Directions should always be constructed in the positive, have happiness and fulfilment at their heart and are to be used for the greater good of all concerned.

Bodymind Directions should always be given as though they were orders. They need to be short and to the point with the most important words prominent.

Remember you may find it more effective to use progressive Bodymind Directions such as *'Calmer and calmer every day'* or *'More and more...'*

Remember also that you can speed up or slow down your responses with phrases like *'Faster please'*, or *'Slowly now'*.

Always give clear Bodymind Directions. If you make a mistake when giving a Bodymind Direction, cancel it and begin again.

**Examples of Bodymind Directions for Daily Inspiration
and Healing**

After you have completed the Tune-in session and the Start-up
Bodymind Directions you can go on to use your own personal Bodymind
Directions. In this section the suggestions for Directions are concerned
with inner calm, emotional and spiritual balance and for your happiness.
Make up your own Bodymind Directions or use some from the examples
below. As before, make sure you leave plenty of time between giving
each Direction to allow your Bodymind Network to make a response.

Select from these suggestions:
Remember: pause after giving each Bodymind Direction.

'Be willing to change.'

'Release the need for negative behaviour patterns in your body,
mind or spirit.'

'Love and approve of yourself.'

'Accept yourself as you are.'

'Feel good about yourself.'

'Be entirely filled with happiness NOW!'

'Feel stronger and stronger every day.'

'More and more positive every day.'

'Remove any negative blockages throughout your entire mind,
body and spirit.'

'Increase the positive input to your body, mind and spirit more and
more.'

'Be aware of and thankful for the good in your life.'

'Fill your entire being with loving kindness towards yourself and
the world.'

Use your Bodymind Directions every day, as often as you can, for
maximum impact and fastest results.

10. Fast Track Communication System

So far, you have been communicating with your Bodymind Network by
giving it instructions, or Bodymind Directions, in order to bring about a

change of some kind. Now you are ready to use the exciting Fast Track Communication System to ask questions of your intuitive higher self. For this you will again use your Bodymind Network to give you physical signals in answer to your questions. With this method you receive 'yes', 'no' or 'maybe' signals in response, so each question needs to be framed so that the answer can be either in the affirmative or negative.

How to Express Your Questions

As already mentioned, in order to receive a clear physical signal, questions need to be expressed so they can generate a 'yes' or 'no' answer. For instance, the question *'How can I organise my day today?'* obviously cannot be answered just with a 'yes' or 'no'. A more satisfactory question on the same theme would be *'Is today a good day for me to ....?'* This question can be clearly understood by your Inner Wisdom which will respond by asking the Bodymind Network to fire the appropriate affirmative or negative response signal.

Questions can be asked about your health, your diet, your physical exercise programme, your emotional life, about choices you are making in your life and spiritual questions, such as your purpose in life. Remember, your inner intuitive self is only interested in doing what is best for you and for those around you. It will never give you answers that will hurt you in any way or be inappropriate from any point of view. Your safety and happiness are its prime concern. The next section gives instructions for this exciting technique.

11. Establishing the 'Yes' and 'No' Signals

Before you are experienced in the Fast Track Communication System it is always best to go through the Tuning-in process and use the Start-up Bodymind Directions. When you are confident in receiving your responses you can omit those stages, but do use them at first.

The signals you are going to use to represent 'yes' and 'no' could be almost any movement from your body that could be repeated again, however, most people find it most convenient to use the following signals as they are simple, easily understood and unobtrusive which makes them easy to use in public situations if required:

The signal for **'yes'** is the raising of your **right** index finger.

The signal for **'no'** is the raising of your **left** index finger.

When you are ready to establish the 'yes and 'no' signals begin the three steps below, as practised before.

FIRST STEP / *Tuning-In*

Find a quiet place where you can be undisturbed for about ten minutes.

Stand with your feet about a foot apart. Look directly ahead, or very slightly down.

Still your body and mind by saying quietly to yourself, 'STOP'. STAND STILL – and WAIT. Allow yourself to relax for one or two minutes, without **doing** anything except becoming more and more aware of your body. If your body wants to move, allow it to do so by itself without interfering in any way. When your body and mind have quietened, and when it feels right to you, begin the Start-up Bodymind Directions.

SECOND STEP / *Give the Start-up Bodymind Directions*

Give the Start-up Bodymind Directions out aloud or just under your breath with a clear, gentle, but firm, voice. **Take your time.** Leave a pause of at least half a minute between each Start-up Bodymind Direction.

Remember you can intensify any response by saying 'more and more' or 'faster than this', or similar phrases of your own as appropriate.

1. **Feel calm and confident.**
(PAUSE AND WAIT, NOTICE ANY RESPONSE)

2. **Smile and feel happy.**
(PAUSE AND WAIT, NOTICE ANY RESPONSE)

3. **Release anything negative from your body, mind and spirit.**
(PAUSE AND WAIT, NOTICE ANY RESPONSE)

4. **Fill your entire being with loving kindness towards yourself and the world.**
(PAUSE AND WAIT, NOTICE ANY RESPONSE)

5. **Feel full of vibrant health and energy. Sparkle with confidence. Glow with joy.**
(PAUSE AND WAIT, NOTICE ANY RESPONSE)

THIRD STEP / *Review*

Take a few moments more to feel and ENJOY the peace and any other sensations you have created.

FOURTH STEP / *Establishing the 'Yes' and 'No' Signals*

Now that you are feeling calm and confident, continue to relax and ask your inner powers for the signal for 'yes'. Do not **consciously** move any part of your body, just pay attention to your body and wait for a response. Remember, the signal for **'yes'** is the raising of your **right** index finger.

First of all, say to your Bodymind Network:

'Be receptive to the 'yes' signal.'

(PAUSE AND WAIT, NOTICE ANY RESPONSE)

Then say:

'Give the signal for 'yes' *now.*'

You should feel an immediate and spontaneous response from your right index finger.

If you are unsure of the response, instruct your Bodymind Network to increase the movement of your finger, say something like 'More than this' or 'A stronger response please'. Do this until you have a really strong signal.

Once you have a good signal, say 'Thank you' to your Bodymind Network.

When you have successfully established your 'yes' signal, establish the 'no' signal in exactly the same way. Remember, the signal for **'no'** is the raising of your **left** index finger.

Say to your Bodymind Network:

'Be receptive to the 'no' signal.'

(PAUSE AND WAIT, NOTICE ANY RESPONSE)

'Give the signal for 'no' *now*.'

As before, you should feel an immediate and spontaneous response from your left index finger.

If you are unsure of the response, instruct your Bodymind Network to increase the movement of your finger, as previously. Do this until you have a really strong signal.

Once you have a good signal, say 'Thank you' to your Bodymind Network.

FIFTH STEP / *Checking the Signals*

To make sure your inner self is absolutely certain of the signals, it is advisable to check them as follows, by testing with asking a question about your name. Note that in order to elicit a 'yes' or 'no' signal it is necessary for the first question to give the *wrong* name, so insert a different name from your own:

Ask,

Is my name ——— (insert a *different* name from your own)?

The signal you receive should be the movement of your left 'no' index finger.

If you do not receive a strong and correct 'no' response to this question, repeat the previous fourth step for establishing the signals.

Then ask,

Is my name ——— (insert your real name)?

The signal you receive should be the movement of your right 'yes' index finger.

If you do not receive a strong and correct 'yes' response to this question, repeat the previous fourth step for establishing the signals.

Remember to thank your inner self after each answer received. This helps to clarify the response mechanism.

NB If you have difficulty in establishing either of the signals, rather than risk further confusion, it may be best to stop for the moment and come back again later in the day, going through the whole process of the Fast Track Communication System from step one onwards.

Regular use of the question and answer system will ensure a continuing strong signal from your Bodymind Network. If you don't use the signal for a while you may find it begins to fade. If so, re-establish the signals by going through all the five steps of the Fast Track Communication System again.

12. Receiving Answers to Your Questions

The wisdom that resides deep inside you has remarkable knowledge and understanding and, because your Inner Wisdom is a force for good, it will never deceive you. You will always receive a true reply to your questions. However, you may find that the response you receive varies from time to time. For instance, sometimes your 'yes' signal may come really quickly and strongly, at other times, your finger may hardly move. This is because your intuitive self is so astute it is able to qualify its answer. For example, in the case of a strong 'yes' response, this means the reply is extremely positive and most definitely in the affirmative. In the instance of a weaker 'yes' signal, your Inner Wisdom may be saying that the answer is 'yes', but there may be aspects of the issue that you should take into account.

The same applies to a negative response, in the case of a strong 'no' signal, this means the reply is most definitely in the negative. If there is a weaker 'no' response, it is likely the answer is 'no', but bear in mind that there may be other factors for you to consider.

On other occasions you may find that both fingers, the 'yes' and 'no' signals, spontaneously move at the same time. This means, 'I don't know', or 'Possibly'. It indicates that your Inner Wisdom has probably not been given enough information to make a judgement as to the reply. Try rephrasing your questions if this happens.

With practice you will soon become accustomed to interpreting what the varying responses mean and you will become more and more adept at phrasing questions so that you receive clear replies.

Examples of Questions To Ask

As mentioned before, questions can be about almost anything, provided they are framed so they can be answered with a 'yes' or 'no' answer. Questions about your health, your food, your exercise programme, your emotional life, choices to make, whether a certain relationship is good for you or more spiritual questions.

Bear in mind that the replies may vary from day to day. For example, if you were asking would it be good for you to go for a swim, it may be good for you today, but not necessarily tomorrow, depending upon your state of health and other variables. Do not doubt the veracity of the answer you receive if it does vary like this. Many factors are being taken into account in the reply you receive.

You also need to be prepared to take on board *any* answer you receive, especially if the answer is contrary to what you had hoped to hear. Remember, your Inner Wisdom always tells the truth and is *always* working with your best interests at heart. So if the response to a question is different from your wishes, be willing to examine your desires again.

Phrase your questions something like these examples:

Would it be good for me to ....

Is .... suitable for me?

Should I ....?

Will .... make me happy?

Getting in touch with yourself at this level is deeply rewarding. This contact with your inner self can be a source of great pleasure, enjoyment and, best of all, comfort in difficult times. The ability to get in touch with your inner truth will support you and give you the confidence to carry on secure in the knowledge that you are being true to yourself in whatever decisions you have to make.

Once you are experienced and assured in your contact with your inner self using the Bodymind Directions and the Fast Track Communication System, you may like to extend your abilities by learning the more advanced communication system to gain even fuller answers to your questions.

13. The Higher Level Communication System

The Higher Level Communication System requires a deeper level of contact with your intuitive self and so requires a slightly different approach from the one used previously. For the Higher Level Communication System you need to be even more relaxed and at peace than when you use the Fast Track Communication System. To achieve this deeper level of relaxation and communion with your inner self you need to sit or lie down in a quiet place for a short while, close your eyes and enjoy a short but deeply peaceful relaxation process.

The slower and deeper breathing during the relaxation process gives the opportunity for the active, logical, 'thinking' left side of your mind to relax, quieten and 'go off duty'. This will allow your Inner Wisdom to tap into the more imaginative right side of your mind, using your incredible imagination bank where millions of images and sensations are stored to produce answers to your questions. The deeper and slower breathing also enables your body to relax completely. Endorphins, the body's own 'feel-good' agents are released and you feel very peaceful and calm. In the Higher Level Communication System you will receive much more information than just a 'yes' or 'no' response to your questions. The way in which you will 'hear' the answers is different again from the Fast Track Communication System where your Bodymind Network produced 'yes' and 'no' finger signals as a response to your questions.

During the deep relaxation your intuitive self will gain the freedom to 'speak' to you. Because it cannot speak in the normal way, it will speak in symbolic form using symbols obtained from your imagination bank. Answers, when they appear to you, may be expressed in colours, images, shapes, sounds, sensations or feelings or sometimes a few words which may be perceived as written words or even spoken words.

Sometimes, you will receive answers with a sensation, a certainty, of just 'knowing', as though a bright light has been shone on the subject. Sometimes the answer may not appear immediately, but will come later, even the next day, during another moment of relaxation and calm, perhaps when you are in a relaxation or meditation session, in the bath, or on a quiet walk. You may then receive your answer 'in a flash' giving sudden insight into how to resolve the issue that concerns you.

At other times you may only perceive the answer in the first thoughts or pictures that come to you as your mind begins to 'wander' away from its attention on your Inner Wisdom. These first thoughts may initially appear to be unrelated to what you wanted to know, however, it is worth considering them as being associated with your answer.

**The Type of Questions to ask the Higher Level
Communication System**

The questions you ask the Higher Level Communication System can be
about almost anything; from your health and your emotional life to more
spiritual questions. As before, the replies from your Inner Wisdom may
change from day to day, depending upon the circumstances at the time
and you also need to be willing to take on board whatever it is your
Inner Wisdom communicates to you. Remember that your Inner Wisdom
only ever speaks the truth and is working with your best interests in
mind. There may be many variable factors your Inner Wisdom is taking
into account, so do not doubt its judgment when you receive an answer.

This time, you can phrase your questions in whatever form you
like, you don't have to consider whether or not they will give a plain
'yes' or 'no' answer. These are examples of the type of questions you
could ask, although, as mentioned, your questions can be about
absolutely anything bar any question which has the intention of bringing
negative qualities into the lives of other people or situations. Your aim
always is to create the highest good for all.

What is blocking me from ....?
How can I overcome ....?
Will it be good for me to ....?
How can I be more successful with ....?
What can I do about ....?

Prior to beginning the session, have your question prepared and make
sure it is expressed clearly and is as short and concise as possible,
then read on to discover how to begin communication with your Inner
Wisdom at a higher level.

14. The Higher Level Communication
System Relaxation Session

You can choose how to use this relaxation process. You could read the
instructions through a few times and then go through the main ideas in
your head, or you could record them on to tape, or you could ask a
friend who is in tune with your aims to read them to you.

Take ten minutes or so to sit or lie down quietly where you won't be disturbed. First of all, just become aware of your breathing and notice the gentle rise and fall of your body as you breathe in and out. Don't alter anything, just notice what is happening for a minute or so. Notice how your body quietens.

On your next outbreath let your breath out through your mouth with a slight sigh and say to yourself, inside your head, 'Relax'.

On the next outbreath, imagine the sigh going down from the top of your head to your abdomen and say to yourself, inside your head, 'Relax'. As you let all the air go, feel relaxation begin to spread through your body.

On the next outbreath, imagine the sigh going down from the top of your head to the soles of your feet and say to yourself, inside your head, 'Relax'. As you let all the air go, feel completely relaxed.

1

Now continue to breathe normally and take your attention around your body, noticing how relaxed it is, and letting the relaxation spread even further and deeper as you become aware of each part – your feet, your legs, abdomen, your lower back, your upper back, your shoulders, your neck and then all around your face and head.

And now that you are relaxed, you are ready to get in touch with your intuitive inner self.

Keep breathing gently, naturally and easily and take your attention to your abdomen. Imagine it is filled with a beautiful warm golden light which spreads and suffuses all around your body. Let this golden light bathe your whole body in healing warmth and relaxation...................Enjoy the feeling.................

And now imagine the light condenses into one tiny ball of bright golden light, all that healing power is concentrated into one spot in your abdomen. Keep your attention on the golden ball of light as this ball of energy can act as the focus for your Inner Wisdom.

And now bring to mind the situation where you feel you need support or help in some way and ask your question, either out aloud or inside your head, making sure it is clearly expressed.

Be open and receptive and willing to allow your Inner Wisdom to suggest images to you. Keep breathing quietly and just allow the question to be there. There's no need to try to **think** of anything. Simply be passive and allow images or sensations to come to you without judging them or reacting in any way.

Take note of the very first images that flash into your mind or sensations you feel in your body, these are most likely to be your answer.

The information may come as a fleeting picture in your mind, a colour, shape or texture, a sound, a voice or a taste. It may be a physical sensation of some kind or just a vague sensation or feeling inside yourself of simply 'knowing' something.

The images produced may sometimes be unclear to you, so if you are not sure what is being said, say, 'Give me more information please', and then wait, without trying to force anything to come, and once again, the first images or sensations that come to you will be the response.

If you are not sure what your image or feeling represents, ask yourself 'What does this remind me of?' Ask yourself if there are any emotions associated with it. Ask yourself how you feel towards it.

Never judge what arrives in your mind. Leave your critical and logical left brain faculties behind, you are tapping into the creative, imaginative right side of your brain. Whatever springs into your imagination is coming from resources deep inside yourself and so trust your intuitive self. Don't rush the process, relax and accept whatever comes. If 'nothing' comes, place your attention on your breathing and the ball of golden energy and spend more time continuing to relax. This intuitive part of you cannot be hurried, it requires a relaxed attitude to flourish. You may find that as soon as you relax and stop trying, an image will present itself. Always remember it is probably the first image that comes to your mind that is the answer to your question, no matter what it is.

With practice and as you continue to use the system, images and sensations will become stronger and clearer, although they are not ever likely to reach the level of being similar to, say, a film on TV. The ideas produced by your inner self usually only come in brief glimpses or flashes.

If you perceive that nothing at all happens, don't worry, just continue to breathe quietly and normally for a little while longer. Be non-judgemental about yourself and about the process. Try again later on or on another day.

When you feel you have come to the end of your session, become aware of the surface beneath you, open your eyes and take in your surroundings. Stretch your fingers, arms and legs and begin movement again, taking with you the feelings of peace and relaxation.

If, this time, you did not receive a reply that satisfied you, do remember, you can always rephrase your question so that it can be answered with either a 'yes' or 'no' signal using the Fast Track Communication System.

Keep on practising the Higher Level Communication System as this type of deeper questioning does take time to perfect. The more you practise the closer you will become to your inner self and its wonderfully supportive resources. Resources which will allow you to transform your life and the lives of those with which you come into contact. Your Inner

Wisdom's guiding and nourishing power will lead you always on to paths of understanding, happiness and joy.

15. The Inner Power of Visualisation

In the Higher Level Communication System you enjoyed a short introduction to the pleasures of the relaxation process. The relaxation had the potential to allow your creative, imaginative side of your mind to come to the fore. The slower and deeper breathing during the relaxation enabled endorphins, your 'feel-good' agents, to be released which brings about feelings of peacefulness and calm. During relaxation your body systems normalise and can begin the healing process. It is most beneficial to develop this ability so that you always have the means of 'recharging your batteries' and bringing about all the benefits from the relaxation session.

Relaxation combined with the inner power of visualisation is a most enjoyable therapy. It is also one of the most exciting and transforming techniques available to us as we can effect healing changes in our bodies and minds. When you use your imagination with skill you can achieve wonders.

To visualise you don't need to be a 'special' kind of person, anyone and everyone has their ability to use their imagination in a creative way. Every time you day-dream, plan a meal, a journey or a holiday you are using visualisation skills. When you plan any of these or other events you will first of all 'see' it in your mind, although you may be unaware that this is what you are doing.

Try these experiments to prove how well you can visualise already:

> **Just notice what happens, don't try to do or see anything. Remember, you can't force images or sensations to come, just allow yourself to relax and see what arises. If you notice something, that's fine, if you don't, that's fine too. Take your time with each item.**

Imagine:

The food you ate at your last meal.

The food you are going to eat at your next meal.

The weight of a football in your hands.

The sound of a whistle blowing.

The taste when sucking a slice of lemon.

The sound of scraping toast.

The feeling of bending down to pick up a piece of paper.

Hearing the rustle of a newspaper opening.

A ship on the horizon of a calm blue sea.

Scuffling through a pile of leaves.

Peeling a banana.

The colour of a dandelion.

The sensation of laughing.

When 'thinking' about each item you will probably have 'seen', 'heard', 'smelt', 'tasted' or 'felt' the response, however momentarily. To 'know' an object or action, you **have** to be able to visualise it, even if you don't recognise that is what you are doing. So, yes, you **can** visualise – very easily, as you found out.

Visualisation is most effective when you are relaxed, and so when practising, it is always best to relax your body and mind first, as you did in the Advanced Two-way Communication System. This sets free your creative forces, allowing you to enjoy 'pictures in your mind' using all your senses, those of sight, touch, taste, smell, hearing. However, this is not something you have to **try** to do. When you relax deeply, it will all come quite naturally and effortlessly. When visualising, some people see or sense objects or events very clearly, almost like a film, but most people just have glimpses or flashes of feelings, pictures or sensations. How**ever** you visualise is right for you. Above all, just relax, have fun and *enjoy* yourself.

Next, there is a wonderfully inspiring and relaxing visualisation which will immerse you totally in feelings of happiness and peace. There is also an extra technique in the visualisation to embed these feelings within you so you can activate them at any time.

16. 'The Key to True Happiness' Visualisation

Visualisation to Enjoy your Full Inner Powers

You can read this visualisation a few times and then take yourself through it from memory, but it is best if you either record it yourself, or ask someone to read it slowly to you. The visualisation can also be obtained from the address at the very end of the book.

Find a quiet place where you can be undisturbed for fifteen minutes or so. Take off your shoes and loosen any tight clothing and sit or lie down where you can be comfortable and warm. Rest your hands at your sides, or on your abdomen without them touching each other.

Become aware of your breathing and just notice the gentle rise and fall of your chest and abdomen as you breathe in and out...................Let your eyes close.

On the next out breath, let your breath out with a slight sigh. ....Aaahhhhhhhhh...........Let your face relax........... Allow yourself a hint of a smile................. The smile will help to relax your whole face................. The sigh will allow your breathing to become deeper and fuller......................... When you breathe in, breathe in through your nose.

On the next outbreath, imagine the sigh going down from the top of your head to the soles of your feet.................... Aaahhhhhhhhh....................... Smile....... Feel the relief as you let the air go and allow all the tension to drain away..............

You feel more and more comfortable and at ease........... Feel your body begin to sink down into the surface beneath you.

And now, travel in your mind down to your feet and say 'Relax' to your feet and allow them to relax even more. Move up to your legs and say 'Relax' to your knees and feel them let go. Now say 'Relax' to your whole legs and feel them relax completely. Say 'Relax' to your lower back and then to your upper back, feel your back become more and more comfortable. Now say 'Relax' to your neck and your head. Allow your neck to be soft and free. Let your head sink down into the support beneath it..........

Move in your mind to your face and say 'Relax' to your face. Allow your forehead to widen and relax .... Notice the muscles letting go.............. Let your eyes soften and relax......... Let all the tiny muscles around your mouth relax, which makes it even easier to gently smile.

Now say 'Relax' to your whole body and just let go completely...............

Your body is soft............your mind is peaceful............you feel totally relaxed and calm..................

This time now is time for you, just for you........time for you to be peaceful and time for you to enjoy the wonderful healing and energising power of your Inner Wisdom.

For this, imagine you are walking down a white sandy beach. The temperature is just right for you. You see the blue, blue sky and the turquoise and green sea. Feel the firm warm sand beneath your feet. You stand by the shore where you hear the waves lapping gently in front of you. In the distance you hear the sound of gulls high above you as they wheel and circle in the blue sky. You sense the light touch of the gentle summer breeze on your skin. It's wonderful to be here by the sea, so peaceful and calm, so fresh and energizing.

It's so tranquil here that you lie down on the beach, shut your eyes and savour the sound of the sea and the warmth of the sun.

You are protected from the sun's rays but can still enjoy its warmth and energy. You hold up your arms to the sun.......... Raise your arms now, in reality, if you wish.............. Really feel the sensation of the warmth of the sun on your arms and hands, feel your fingertips tingle with its glittering energy. You feel as though between your hands you have a ball of dancing sunlight, each particle pulsating, shimmering and sparkling with pure happiness, pure energy, pure love.............

Holding the ball of sunlight, slowly, slowly bring your hands down again until your hand and the sunlight are resting on your abdomen. Feel the comfort, warmth and happy energy from the sunlight spread inside you.

Imagine all this energy and sunlight concentrated down into a tiny golden ball. This ball of pure light vibrates and shimmers with energy, happiness and love. This, indeed, is your real Inner Power, a wonderful place for all your Inner Wisdom to reside.

See the way the sparkling light radiates and grows with every breath you take, see how the happiness grows and grows inside you. The ball of light grows bigger and bigger until it radiates pure happiness and love. And now with every breath you take, the happiness, love and energy spread right around your body, filling every part from head to toe. The feelings grow and grow, ever expanding. Your body is bathed inside with wonderful glowing golden light and your body is filled with serenity, love and real happiness. This golden light is healing, rejuvenating and energising, feel its subtle power working in you.

Imagine that there is so much radiant happiness and love within you that it overflows and spreads outside to surround your body to create a wonderful golden aura...... With every breath you take you breathe out more and more power, love and energy. You are filled and surrounded with so much pure happiness and love that it can now spreads out to the wider world. You breathe happiness, warmth and sparkling energy out to the wider world.

Everyone you will meet is touched with your personal warmth, happiness and love which radiates out from you. It gives you pleasure and delight to share the way you feel.

Now that you are at the peak of feeling so wonderful, serene and happy, press your first finger and thumb together to anchor the feelings you have created. This will fix the experience of pure happiness and joy to the signal. From now on you will be able to feel this way again at any time you like just by using the anchor signal.

Take a few moments more to enjoy the peace and serenity and then take these feelings of peace and tranquillity, of being healthy, happy and confident, back with you as you slowly become aware of the surface beneath you and, when you are ready, come back to the room.

Lie quietly for a few moments more to appreciate the feelings of happiness, joy and serenity that are always within you......... and now you know how to contact these feelings again at any time, either with this whole visualisation, or by pressing your anchor signal.

In ten minutes or so, test your anchor signal by pressing your finger and thumb together, and feel the wonderful feelings from this visualisation once again. Every time you use the signal or go through the visualisation the feelings will become stronger and stronger.

When you are ready, stretch your fingers and toes, feel peaceful and calm yet alert and ready to go about your day, taking all these feelings with you.

After enjoying this visualisation remember to practise firing your anchor signal, try it throughout the day to rekindle the feelings of happiness and joy.

17. Unleash Your Inner Powers NOW!

Your Inner Wisdom is one of the the most important of the Five Feel-good Factors because of its far-reaching and overall influence for good and also its potential for creative interactment with your Bodymind Network. With the correct Bodymind Directions, you can use it to initiate and support your healing processes and you will discover that with practice and repetition, you can create remarkable therapeutic results. You can direct the life-affirming power of your Inner Wisdom to initiate transformation in every part of your being, body, mind and spirit. By developing the ability to converse with your Inner Wisdom you have access to the deep and true intelligence that lies within you.

Now that you are open to the possibilities of its extensive powers, you can truly effect many desirable changes in your life, all of which will lead you to real happiness, peace of mind and fulfilment. Using your inner powers will bring you more confidence and focus and you will notice that many aspects of your life show signs of beneficial and pleasing change.

Your inner powers are phenomenal and can sustain you in limitless areas of your life, therefore be ever mindful of the possibilities of your inner creative ability. You will then begin to live in harmony with your true self; to live your dreams.

The power of your Inner Wisdom can shine the bright light of health, happiness and compassion into the darkest corners at the darkest hours. Nurture and cherish its presence and it will nurture and cherish you in return in ever increasing levels of abundance.

Remain in tune with your Inner Wisdom, using its power to stay 'on line', on the golden path of happiness, success and increasing good health. Nourish and cultivate your inner powers and your whole life will be enriched; you will sparkle with vitality and energy. Your happiness and success will be assured. So, be alive to the possibilities within yourself and unleash your inner powers **NOW.**

18. Review

1. When you live your life guided by your Inner Wisdom you are on the path to abundant happiness and health.

42

2. Your mind and body are one, linked together inextricably in the Bodymind Network. The Bodymind Network is within the influence of your inner powers. Use the transforming Bodymind Directions to make the changes you desire (7–10).

3. Use the Bodymind Directions every day to promote happiness, inner calm, emotional and spiritual balance and better health (11–13).

4. With the Fast Track Communication System and the Higher Level Communication System you can benefit from the intuitive wisdom of your inner self for advice and problem-solving (14–15).

5. Enjoy maximum input to your happiness with the beautiful 'Key to True Happiness Visualisation' (17).

1

Find inner peace

1. Find Inner Peace

The second Feel-good Factor is the creation of inner peace for yourself. When you have a fundamental source of peace and calm, you gain immense inner strength; you gain insight, a powerful sense of yourself and the ability to master your own internal forces of conflict. With inner peace in your heart and mind you are able to cope more easily with life's daily stresses and strains, finding creative solutions to challenges as they arise.

You find this quality of inner peace in the power, strength and energy of the masters of martial arts. Their energies and concentration come directly from a centre of calm and peace, as, also, does creativity. True creativity does not come from hyperactivity, high adrenaline and panic as deadlines approach, it flows instead from that same centre of inner peace. Therefore, when you are blessed with being in a state of inner peace your accomplishments can be greater; and inner peace, of course, goes hand in hand with happiness itself.

To find inner peace you need to 'come into the present moment', which is the only place you can ever find peace of mind and body. When you discover your own inner peace it is like 'coming home' to yourself. It's a place where you feel totally comfortable, completely safe and absolutely at one with yourself.

Another factor for inner peace is having strong, loving and accepting relationships with others. There is always a choice here, you are free to criticize both yourself and others, but why criticize when the capacity to understand and forgive brings so much love and peace into not only your life, but theirs also? When you understand and forgive you align your mind and emotions into greater harmony. Inner peace comes from forgiveness; as you forgive, you are healed and you create a huge surge in your inner strengths of perception, understanding and loving kindness. So, make peace, make peace with yourself and with everyone around you.

There are simple but powerful techniques in this section to show you the way to attain this inner peace which are adaptations of methods which have been in use for thousands of years. There is also a wonderful technique which is guaranteed to keep you smiling, not only on the outside, but on the inside too, so that your whole body feels happy and peaceful. Also included is a simple technique to maximise your happiness and to make the most of the tiniest scrap of happiness during your day, nurturing and cherishing it so that it grows boundlessly, allowing you to pass on your blessings to others.

However busy you are the techniques which follow take very little of your time so they can easily be built into your day. The techniques will bring you inner peace in very simple and easy ways. Do use them, they are the essence of this second feel-good factor and are totally, reliably effective in changing the way you feel. Inner peace can be yours starting now.

2. Your Body Speaks For You

You don't always have to tell other people how you are feeling, they can guess for themselves because your body language says it for you. For example, when you feel depressed, it is mirrored in your posture; you tend to shrink down into yourself, your head is more bowed and your face droops, reflecting your negative feelings. When you are feeling happy and outgoing, you walk with a bounce, your head is held high and there is a smile on your lips, a sparkle in your eye. Once again, your feelings have been reflected in your body language. The same applies to other emotions, think of someone who is angry or someone who is frightened and you will immediately receive an image of their facial expression and their body shape. Think of someone whose expression is calm and gentle, who moves quietly with grace and whose voice is well modulated and pleasantly pitched and you will be looking at someone who knows all about living in a state of inner peace.

Now, the point about body language is of interest to you because the same is true *in reverse. Your body posture influences your feelings.* In other words, the way you move and hold your body can directly affect the way you feel emotionally. Try this quick experiment to prove it for yourself.

Do these exercises wholeheartedly and with a genuinely open mind.

Just notice first of all how you are feeling at the moment. Make a mental note of your emotion.

And now, notice how you are holding your body and what is the expression on your face?

Even in a very small way, do the two relate at all? Whatever you are feeling and doing, just notice.

Next, let your shoulders sag down and forwards, let your head drop down and look down to the ground, let your face droop, your mouth go down at the corners.

How do you feel now?

Notice any way in which your body posture has affected how you feel.

Now, quickly straighten up and raise your head. Raise your arms as though to embrace the sun and the sky, look up, relax your eyes and mouth and smile.

And now how do you feel?

Again, notice any difference this body posture has made to your emotions.

Although you may not have felt in either a particularly negative or positive frame of mind when you began, the different body languages you used in this experiment would have had some impact upon your emotions, however slight and fleeting. When you positioned your body in a certain way your emotions followed what was being described by your body. Probably you noticed quite a contrast between the two body postures and your emotions. When your posture displayed 'I feel depressed', you probably felt somewhat helpless and downhearted; when your pose suggested 'I feel strong, happy and joyous', you would immediately have felt your mood change and lift.

As you will be beginning to see, this facility to *act* an emotion and then, as a result, *feel* the emotion, is of great importance to you in your quest for happiness. By acting out the emotion in your posture, you encourage your Bodymind Network into producing the corresponding feeling.

Most importantly, the act of *smiling* alone was the most important component in producing the emotion of 'happiness' in your acting experiment. To explain: when you smile, the muscles in your face relax, your face widens, your forehead relaxes and all the tiny muscles around your eyes also let go and relax. These facial muscles help to regulate the flow of blood to your brain and allowing them to relax into a smile enables the blood to flow more freely to your brain. Frowning or pulling the mouth down has, of course, the opposite effect and causes tension and stress with its associated negative effects. However, when you smile, all the cells of your brain are then bathed with an increased supply of oxygen and nutrients which enables them to function more efficiently. In this way your brain power is improved and the production of endorphins, your body's natural 'feel-good' agent or 'happy medicine', is initiated. Best of all, smiling takes years off you, it makes you both look and feel much younger.

Endorphins are part of the 'relaxation response' which is an inborn response enabling your whole system, including the immune system, to function more effectively. Endorphins also help to maximise your natural healing processes and, in addition, act as painkillers, damping down pain anywhere in your body. Emotionally, when endorphins are flowing freely, you feel more relaxed and at ease with the world and yourself, you are able to function calmly and respond to challenging situations serenely, using your intellect and logic instead of emotional reasoning. As you can see, a simple smile can be the beginning of a wonderful ascendancy to a higher level of being for yourself and for the way you handle your life and respond to the world. As you discovered with the experiments, you don't even have to *feel* like smiling, the very act of deliberately putting a smile on your face sends a 'happiness message' to your subconscious mind which automatically passes it on to *you* and your reality; happiness becomes true for you and when you feel happy, you feel that elusive quality of inner peace.

This quality of inner peace need no longer be elusive. See how, over the next few pages, you can ensure you live with peace in your heart, mind and body.

3. 'Breathe and Smile' Mantra

To guarantee your success and to be most effective, you need to build a structure around using your smile. This structure will allow you to hold the 'happiness response' within your own control and ensure it is 'kick started' at regular intervals during your busy day which will encourage the free flowing of those wonderful endorphins and, as a consequence, the build up of happiness and peace within you. This simple technique alone has the capability to transform your whole life. It also reaches into the lives of those around you. As your aura of serenity and inner peace touches them, they cannot help but respond in a like way.

When you smile it is an affirmation of your decision to live a life of peace and happiness. When you begin the day with a smile, you are setting the tone for the day; you are sending yourself messages that you approach the day with gentleness and joy. The simple 'mantra' of Bodymind Directions below brings you right into the present moment, where peace and joy always reside. Remember, happiness and peace are not at some place, some time in the future, they are always and only right here, right now.

The 'Breathe and Smile' Mantra links your breathing with some Bodymind Directions, making it a very powerful tool. This is how endorphins are produced by the two elements of the 'Breathe and Smile' Mantra:

1. With the 'Breathe and Smile' Mantra you become aware of your breathing pattern. With more heightened awareness of your breathing, you will find it becomes deeper and slower. This type of deeper and slower breathing is very calming and relaxing in itself and encourages the flow of endorphins. Your body and your mind begin to relax into peace.

2. The Bodymind Directions you give instructing yourself to smile and to feel peaceful have the same effect, thus doubling up on the production of endorphins and on the feelings of peace, happiness and tranquillity. Remember, you don't even have to *feel* like smiling. The message is passed on via your Bodymind Network

and your body automatically responds allowing you to feel the
benefit of the relaxation and calmness.

Try this now.............. there's no need to lie down or even to sit
down, nor to shut your eyes, unless you want to. You can smile
and feel peaceful wherever you are, whatever you're doing.
Repeat this simple but powerful exercise over and over. Try it for
three or four minutes and see what an incredible difference it
makes to you.

Breathing Pattern		Bodymind Direction
As you breathe	IN	'Breathe in.........
As you breathe	OUT	and smile............'
As you breathe	IN	'Feel peaceful.....
As you breathe	OUT	and calm...........'

Repeat this sequence as many times as you like.

Notice how you feel now compared with how you felt before you
began...................

With the 'Breathe and Smile' Mantra you have been practising a simple
form of meditation. Yes, meditation is as simple and pleasurable as
this, not a difficult or mysterious thing to do at all. There is more about
meditation later on.

While you are giving the Bodymind Directions and placing your
attention on your breath and your smile, you are firmly rooted in the
present moment which is the only place you can find happiness and
peace. During this time you are also stilling your mind. Your thoughts
slow down and instead of your mind chasing thought after thought of the
past or the future, it slows, comes into the present and leaves any
anxieties and worries behind. You are truly resting your mind and as
your mind rests, your body becomes quieter and more peaceful.

When you come into the present in this refreshing, energising
way you are cherishing and nurturing yourself in a deeply healing way
and are in touch with your own peace. This wonderful experience is

available to you at any time, day or night. Use this simple 'Breathe and Smile' exercise as often as you can in your day. It is guaranteed to make you feel wonderful and you will then be able to continue with what you were doing revitalized and filled with peace and contentment.

The next section develops the idea of incorporating the 'Breathe and Smile' Mantra into your daily activities.

4. Other Opportunities for the 'Breathe and Smile' Mantra

Wake Up with Inner Peace

What a wonderful way to start the day! Let the 'Breathe and Smile' Mantra be the very first thing you do in the morning as soon as you awake to give you a really peaceful start to the day. This simple act can transform your whole day as it reaffirms that you come to the new day in joy and equanimity. With this gentle approach to the day you will find time expands. Normally, when we rush about in a hurry time contracts and there never seems to be enough. With this new approach, there will be plenty of time, as the more gently and sensitively you move around, the easier tasks are to perform. You don't make mistakes, drop things or rush around in a panic searching for lost objects. Calmness banishes chaos. Let inner peace reign with the 'Breathe and Smile' Mantra *every* day.

Walk with Inner Peace

A lovely way to use the 'Breathe and Smile' Mantra is to practice whilst you are walking. For the exercise you will need to walk a little more slowly than normal and co-ordinate your steps to your breathing. You may find you take three steps, or perhaps four, with each out and in breath. You may find you need an extra step for breathing out, perhaps three for breathing in and four for breathing out; find out which rhythm suits you personally. As you walk, repeat your words to yourself and be more aware than usual of your feet's contact with the ground and of the sights around you. You will find you begin to notice and appreciate tiny details of nature that you may have missed before. A bud as it first breaks open, minute insects scurrying about their work, the dew on a flower or a beautiful sky. *Enjoy* your 'smiling walk'.

Talk with Inner Peace

One of the causes of most stress to us is the telephone. Even when silent, when it's not demanding your attention with its strident call, it can be a source of some anxiety; perhaps you are waiting for some news or a special call, perhaps you have to ring someone you don't particularly want to speak to, perhaps the phone bill is far more expensive than you had realised.

When the phone does ring, it may be a longed-for call for you to enjoy but it may also be bringing you news you don't really want to hear. At work, it may be that it never seems to stop ringing, with one demand after another being made upon you.

To handle this, instead of rushing impatiently to the phone when it rings, take a moment before you snatch at the receiver to think of your breath and to bring that smile to your face. It will only take a second to use the first part of the 'Breathe and Smile' Mantra as below, and then when you speak to the person at the other end of the line the calmness, equanimity and peace will be reflected in the quality of your voice. Your smile and your peace will be transferred to the person at the other end of the line resulting in a much more relaxed and positive conversation. As well as counteracting stress, smiling is extremely catching!

When the phone rings, let it ring for one ring longer than usual and take the opportunity to use just the smile element of the 'Breathe and Smile' Mantra:

IN	'Breathe in.........
OUT	and smile............'

Other Opportunities for the 'Breathe and Smile' Mantra

You can use the 'Breathe and Smile' Mantra on many other occasions, perhaps when you are caught in a heavy traffic jam and not making the progress you would like. Instead of making it a stressful and frustrating experience, take the opportunity to smile and find the peace within you. Other occasions to use the 'Breathe and Smile' Mantra might be when you are in a queue, a lift, or on an escalator, train or bus. There are so many occasions when this wonderful tool will revitalise you, 'earth' you and give you inner peace.

You could build the 'Smiling Mantra' into your daily activities by taking advantage of particular events during your day to prompt the use of the technique. Perhaps when you visit the bathroom, turn your PC on, wait for the kettle to boil, or when chopping vegetables; indeed, *whenever* you are engaging in a routine activity use it as a cue to introduce the technique. With practice you can use the technique during meetings, whilst you are shopping or filling the car with petrol. In fact, virtually wherever you are, whatever you're doing you can use the 'Smiling Mantra'. Use it often and inner peace will be yours.

5. Body Smiling

To continue with the theme of smiling, try 'Body Smiling'. This imaginative exercise will give you a deeper relaxation and bring inner peace and healing to your whole body and mind.

Take as long as you like for this exercise, anything between 5–20 minutes. Read it through first, then take yourself through the whole exercise or ask someone who is in tune with you to read it slowly to you.

2

Make yourself comfortable, where you won't be disturbed and sit or lie down with your shoes off and any tight clothing loosened. Allow yourself plenty of time as you think about each part of your body.

First of all, just become aware of your breathing and notice your body as it gently rises and falls as you breathe in and out.

On your next out-breath let your breath out through your mouth with a slight sigh. With the sigh, allow yourself the hint of a smile to relax your face. Breathe in through your nose.

On your next out-breath, imagine the sigh going down from the top of your head to your abdomen. As you let the air out, just let go.........

On your next out-breath, imagine the sigh going down from the top of your head to the tips of your toes. As you let the air go, feel the last drop of tension drain away.......

Now continue to breathe normally.

Take your attention now to your abdomen. With each in-breath, imagine your breath filling it with warmth, peace and relaxation. Feel your abdomen being bathed in that warmth and peace and sense that all the tiny cells in that area are happy and working to the peak of their ability in the interests of your health and well being. Imagine each tiny cell is smiling and happy as it goes about its work. Now imagine that the whole area is one big smile of happiness from one side of your abdomen to the other. Stay with this image for as long as you like before moving on to another part of your body.

2

Use the same ideas for your back, your neck, your face and even the inside of your head would benefit from this very special attention. Then apply similar ideas to any other area of your body that you feel would find the technique enriching.

When you have finished you will be completely relaxed and filled with peace and the sensation of a smiling and happy body. Then lie still for a while and enjoy this feeling of being bathed in a wonderful warm and happy glow for as long as you like.

When you are ready to begin movement again, stretch out and gently begin to go about your day, taking the feelings you have created with you. Keep a gentle smile on your face and know that your whole body is smiling with you.

Treat yourself to this beautiful visualisation as often as you can to give yourself a 'smile bath'. In fact, going through the visualisation while you *are* in the bath is a very good idea. Try it and bring real peace to your whole body and mind.

6. Maximise Your Inner Peace and Happiness

An excellent way to foster your inner peace and happiness is to become more aware of the moments of peace and happiness you have in your life already. You can easily maximise your happiness with the following technique which is designed systematically to seek out every ounce of happiness from each moment of pleasure, contentment, peace and joy in your life. At first you may need to seek very diligently until you become accustomed to the idea as most of us are unused to focusing on the good in our lives and in the world around us. However, once you begin you will find it becomes easier and easier each day. With a growing sensitivity to the good and the positivity in your life you will experience more and more joy because happiness attracts yet more happiness; coming from a centre of peace encourages peace to grow in others, its ripples spreading ever outward. This technique will only take a few minutes of your time each day, so start today and see how your life begins to transform.

2

Maximise your inner peace each evening by taking just a few minutes before you go to bed to gather every scrap of peace and happiness from your day, no matter how slight. At the beginning, it's a good idea to write each detail in a special notebook or in your diary. After a while it will become second-nature to you to glean these moments of peace and happiness and you can then just enjoy each re-lived moment in your mind without writing them down.

As you think back through your day, be kind to yourself, don't linger with any thoughts about challenges you may have faced during the day, unless it is to congratulate yourself on the way in which you handled them. Be drawn like a magnet instead to moments where you have been successful and positive.

Write down all the blessings, achievements and good moments from your day. Note every time you felt, even for a moment, a sense of being content with what you had done, seen, heard, smelt or touched: a welcome letter, a compliment, a visit, the smell of a flower, the colour and texture of some fruit, a smile from a neighbour or friend, the style in which you handled a situation, a smile at yourself in the mirror, a pleasant phone call, a beautiful view: note absolutely everything that enhanced your day and made your heart sing. Like a cat being stroked, luxuriate in each moment, however tiny, take joy in their full detail, seeing, hearing, feeling, tasting and smelling everything about them once again.

As you think of each item, deliberately **smile** gently and allow the happy moment to settle around and within you like a golden glow. These small moments of pleasure are very precious and add up to feelings of great satisfaction, inner peace and joy when gathered together.

2

Read through your list and at the very end write,

'You **deserve** to have inner peace and to be happy.'

Repeat this Bodymind Direction over and over to yourself saying it with real feeling until it begins to sound natural and right to you. You **do** deserve to have inner peace and be happy, just as you are, right now, without doing anything else but to be here.

Re-read your list often and either add to it every day or begin a new one each day.

Your inner peace and happiness will grow as you gather together all those precious golden moments from your life and will surely be returned to you as your own inner peace and happiness is mirrored back to you.

You can extend the exercise to gain an ever growing abundance of warmth, peace and love within yourself.

The joy, warmth and glow you feel when you have read through your list of special moments can be multiplied by not keeping it for yourself but by giving it away! When you give love, warmth and comfort, you don't give your own feelings away. As you give to someone else, your feelings not only remain with you but they grow deeper and deeper as you think of that person.

And so, think of someone who has need of your wonderful gift and then imagine that the gift of all your feelings of love, happiness and peace are transmuted into a shimmering golden glow. Now imagine that you send this shimmering radiance to the other person and, in your mind's eye, see it sparkling, shining and glowing around them, surrounding them with your loving warmth, peace and comfort.

Notice how you now feel even stronger sensations of peace, love and contentment than before. Enjoy how your feelings have been multiplied with your act of giving.

Maximise your inner peace and happiness often with this wonderful exercise.

7. Just Being

One of the techniques with the potential for the most profound outcome is the practice of meditation. When you used the previous 'Breathe and Smile Mantra' you were already enjoying a simple form of meditation. Meditation has its roots in many of the world's religions where it is used to bring spiritual enlightenment. However, you don't have to be religious to benefit from its many outcomes, such as improved physical, mental and emotional health.

The practice of meditation goes back thousands of years as part of religions such as Christianity, Buddhism and Hinduism. Meditation really took off in the 1960s when it was introduced into this country by the Indian guru, Maharishi Mahesh Yogi. He introduced a popular version called Transcendental Meditation which uses a mantra as a focus to keep the mind from wandering. The mantra could be either a religious word or sound, or a more earthly word, such as 'love' or 'peace'. Another form of meditation is the Buddhist 'mindfulness' meditation where you become 'mindful' of your breath, letting go of thoughts as they arise. Yet another form is the Buddhist 'loving kindness' meditation which has as a focus a happy occasion from the past. This, you then bring into the present to enjoy the happy feelings again, firstly by you, and then extended out to others, with multiplying feelings of loving kindness. These methods form the foundation of many modern meditation practices, elements of which you will recognise in the forms of meditation in this book.

Modern meditation practice encompasses a number of different techniques which are used to relax your body, still your mind and bring you into a state of deep inner peace. The practice of meditation ensures you are firmly rooted in the present moment, it brings you into deep relaxation, allowing breathing to slow, your blood pressure to drop and your body to relax and restore itself. Meditation aims to unite body and mind into a state which allows your natural healing processes to be freed with the consequence that minor aches, pains and ailments have the potential to disappear. Your mind remains calm and clear, in a state of 'relaxed awareness'. This calm yet alert state produces feelings of deep peace and inner harmony. You feel as if you have 'come home to yourself', to a place of deepest calm.

You feel this sense of calmness and tranquillity because the dominant left-hand side of your brain has slowed down. This is the area of your brain which deals with analytical and rational thought and which produces almost constant 'mental chatter'. Thoughts and thinking take you away from the present moment into the realms of fantasy, the past and the future. All places of unreality and illusion.

When you are 'lost' in your thoughts you don't pay full attention to whatever you are doing or to the world around you. You may spend much of the day on 'automatic pilot' in a half-awake daze, your mind filled with random or worry thoughts about what has been, what might have been or what may or may not happen in the future. These thoughts can be a major source of negative emotions that can affect your health and your mental and emotional equilibrium. Days spent like this leave you with a deep feeling of dissatisfaction. You can't stop your thoughts, as it is the function of your mind to produce thoughts. However, you can learn to take hold of your own power and let the thoughts go, instead of reacting automatically to them. With your centre of calm and peace you will be able to cope more easily with any stresses in your life.

Practising meditation on a daily basis leads to greater happiness, health, inner peace, heightening your self knowledge and your perception of the world around you. When you meditate you discover a whole new and exciting world – your own inner self. The journey of meditation is one of self-discovery and enormous personal growth. You can build a whole new positive attitude towards yourself based on the discovery of your own inner peace.

8. The Benefits of 'Just Being'

Meditation has a balancing effect on your brain and allows the right-hand side of your brain (which is associated with creativity, intuition and emotion) to come to life and flourish. Being in balance in this way is your natural, inborn way of being. The benefits of practising any form of meditation are wide ranging. They lead to greater happiness and self-awareness, as well as more tolerance towards yourself, others and the situations in which you find yourself. You feel more awake and alert, and yet maintain a relaxed attitude of body and mind. You feel energised and your concentration and creativity are enhanced, leading to greater productivity. You become more incisive and find rational yet imaginative solutions to any problems more easily.

Even though your mind may be in turmoil on occasions as the result of some predicament, with meditation you learn how to respond to situations and events in a calm manner owing to the greater access you have to your inner powers and strengths. You feel in control of your life and, above all, you know you have a central well of inner peace and strength that you can tap into at any time. You discover the real you, the peaceful, calm and loving you that lies beneath the superficial surface. You learn to value yourself as you are, accepting yourself and feeling that you are good enough just as you are right now.

Your health improves as all your bodily functions improve, including your immune and natural healing systems. This means many ailments have the potential to be overcome, from depression and insomnia to reduced migraine, heart problems and asthma attacks.

2

You discover that when the days don't disappear altogether in day-dreaming you become more aware and free to take pleasure from the smallest detail of your life. Microscopic but awesomely wonderful facets of Nature are revealed to you: the delicate lines of the petal of a flower, the tracery of bare branches against the sky, the colour of autumn leaves, the breathtaking beauty of a newly unfurled leaf, the smell of recently cut grass, birdsong as a new day is greeted, man-made artefacts such as a stunning sculpture, a thought-provoking photograph, the pleasing lines of a building. All these and more become apparent to you as your senses are expanded. You enjoy a new relationship with all around you and come to understand and be comfortable with your place in the natural world.

When you recognise and appreciate moments such as these you are fully alive, calm and peaceful. These moments help to balance out your day, making all the difference between a hectic, rushed day and a more content and satisfying one. Your relationships improve as you become more aware of both yourself and the outside world and learn to accept things as they are. As you develop a sense of yourself and your connectedness with the world around you, your life becomes fuller and more enjoyable. You become content to be who you are, as you are. The deeper your practice of meditation goes, the more you move beyond all the desires and cravings of the world outside to the true centre of yourself, to that immutable and steadfast core of stillness and serenity. Inner peace is yours.

Meditation is open to everyone, you can regard it as a gift – a gift from yourself to yourself. A gift to yourself which strangely becomes a gift somehow for the benefit of others as your ability to relate to them is enhanced. When you learn to listen with attention to others you come to understand them and why they have acted in a particular way. Finally you come to forgive them for not being what you thought they ought to be and to forgive yourself for thinking they have to be something you wanted them to be. With understanding and forgiveness comes compassion and a growing sense of loving kindness towards them and yourself.

We can all learn how to meditate and gain all these wonderful benefits. All you need do is to sit quietly for a few minutes twice a day. During this special time you don't *do* anything, meditation is a state of not-doing, not-trying, not-endgaining, just *being* and letting whatever happens to happen. If you strive for peace, creativity or health these elements will elude you. They are far more likely to come if you relax your attitude into one of 'allowing' and letting go of actively desiring or struggling for whatever it is you think you want. You may then be surprised at the many beneficial outcomes of your practice of meditation. Some effects may be immediately noticed, others will come later as you realise how you have changed progressively in subtle and profound ways.

9. A Simple Meditation Exercise

For your first experience of meditation it's best to have an attitude of 'Let's see what happens'. So, try this simple meditation exercise now and just notice what happens when you close your eyes and allow your body to settle.

> Find a quiet place where you will be uninterrupted for about five minutes. Sit in a comfortable position, close your eyes and become aware of your breath. Notice the slight rise and fall of your body as it flows in and out. Place your attention **only** on your breath and take no notice of any sounds from inside or outside the room or any sensations from the rest of your body. The aim is to focus, for the allotted time, only on your breath and its in-flow and out-flow.
>
> Start this meditation now.

Assessing the Meditation Exercise

You may have found the seemingly simple task of focusing on your breath surprisingly complex. If you noticed many thoughts and sensations intruding as you tried to maintain your attention on your breath, don't worry, this is perfectly normal. Once you understand a little more about it, you will see why the practice of meditation is so beneficial and learn the best way to approach the thoughts and sensations. It's all about attitude.

The Attitude To Take Towards Meditation

The particular quality of your attitude to the meditation is what makes the crucial difference. It will all fall into place as I explain.

> The central factor in meditation is *the quality of the way in which you bring your attention back to your focus*. Your attention needs to be brought gently and calmly back, with no impatience or criticism of yourself. You do this over and over, as many times as it happens. Just noticing the intruding thoughts, then letting them go, noticing, then letting go. You may have to do this many, many times, it doesn't matter. *This is the normal pattern of meditation and happens to everyone*. This is, in a way, the whole point of meditation, your mind *will* wander. You are not trying to control your mind or to stop the thoughts from occurring, your job is just to notice the thoughts and let them go, not get hooked up into following them. You are learning to stand back from the thoughts and, therefore, your emotions. This leads to greater emotional stability where you are not so likely to become swept away with negative feelings. As you continue to practice you will become used to the idea of thoughts intruding and then letting them go.

Developing this attitude leads directly to growing feelings of understanding, compassion and tolerance towards yourself and, of course, leads you to your wonderfully calm centre of inner peace.

The Nature of Thought

The consciousness behind the thoughts, the consciousness that has the ability to interrupt thoughts and to direct you away from them and back to your focus is the 'real' you. The thoughts you think are produced by your mind. It is the function of your mind to produce thoughts, in the same way it is the function of your stomach to produce digestive juices or the function of a hair cell to grow hair. The consciousness behind the thoughts, however, has the power to choose whether or not to follow those thoughts. With this understanding about the nature of thoughts, you can appreciate that you do not have to be at the mercy of what you think. It is your choice whether you follow them or not. This is not just applicable during the practice of meditation but at any time of the day when you catch yourself following a particular train of thought that is not profitable to you. *You* have the power and the authority to dismiss those thoughts or choose not to follow them. Even disturbing thoughts will pass more quickly if you can accept them as they are – just thoughts, that you need not respond to if you so choose.

When you meditate, the less you 'try' or worry about how you are doing the better. All that matters is that you are involved in the practice of meditation on a daily basis. Please don't be impatient, judgemental or critical of yourself or your 'progress', instead approach meditation with an open mind and an attitude of 'I'll just go with it and see what comes about'.

Now discover for yourself the benefits of this wonderful method for gaining inner peace. Read the next section and then, to begin with, set aside just five minutes at a time to practice. That's all you need to come home to your own inner peace and to benefit from all that flows from it.

10. Meditation for Inner Peace

The idea of 'just sitting' and 'being' sounds very simple. However, when you do 'just sit' there is nothing to distract you (as you found in the previous exercise) and you become immediately conscious of one thought after another tumbling from your mind. It is all too easy unconsciously to begin to follow those thoughts and so become led away from your sense of self. Your mind's function is to produce these thoughts, one after another. *Your* function, during meditation, is to allow the thoughts to pass through your mind without you becoming either caught up with them or reacting to them.

To do this you need a simple focus for your mind. This focus will also serve the purpose of giving you something to return to when, as is inevitable, your mind begins to wander. Two of the most popular sources of focus are repeating a mantra of a word or sound, or placing your attention on an external object such as a candle flame or a flower. On this occasion you are going to use your breath as it flows in and out as a focus. Meditation is not a 'heavy' time but one which needs to be approached with lightness, compassion and with a sense of loving kindness towards yourself.

Begin, as follows, with a five minute practice and gradually build up to fifteen to twenty minutes, twice a day, preferably. With experience you will find you can sense for how long you have been meditating.

Find a quiet, comfortable place where you can be undisturbed for a short while. Although you don't have to sit in any particular way, such as in the 'lotus' position or cross legged, do sit as straight as you can, but without causing any extra muscular tension which would distract you. You should be comfortable, but in a position where you remain alert. Try sitting upright in a straight-backed chair, both feet flat on the floor and your hands resting lightly on your thighs, palms facing upwards, not touching each other.

Close your eyes and breathing through your nose take your attention to your breath. Don't try to interfere with its pattern in any way, just observe it as it flows in and out. Notice how your body begins to quieten. If any areas of your body feel tense, take your attention to the area and as you breathe out allow the area to relax and soften.

Don't try to alter your breathing pattern in any way, just breathe naturally and as you continue with the meditation you will slowly feel more and more peaceful and serene.

There's no need to try to force yourself to concentrate, instead have a sense of lightness about the way you bring your mind to rest on the words. As soon as you notice your attention has wandered and is no longer on your breath, just note the thoughts that have distracted you and, without criticising yourself, let the thoughts go, let them float away and gently bring your attention back to your breath.

Continue like this for your allotted time, focusing on your breath, then letting go of thoughts and sensations as they arise. If you feel uncomfortable, rather than continue to be distracted by it, gently move with your full attention on your body whilst you do so

2

and then return your mind to your breath once you are more comfortable again. If the discomfort persists, place your full attention on the area and gently breathe in and out of it until the sensations dissipate. If you try to ignore the discomfort or pull away from it your muscles will tend to tighten up around it which will naturally increase the painful sensations. So, take the opposite path and take your attention right into the discomfort which will relax it.

When it is time for you to end the meditation, bring your attention back to everyday thoughts, open your eyes and remain quite still for a few moments longer while you enjoy the feelings you have created. Then stretch gently and take the feelings of peace and calmness with you as you gradually begin activity again.

Your Thoughts

For the first few minutes of the meditation you can expect thoughts to crowd in demanding your attention but your attention gradually will become more stable and as it does so the benefits will increase accordingly. Maintaining your attention during meditation can be quite tiring which is why you need to build up the time gradually. If you find your meditation practice is becoming 'heavy', try sitting with a gentle smile on your lips, this will act as an instruction to your Bodymind Network to lighten up and relax.

Notice the type of thoughts that recur during your practice. You may find you keep returning to particular issues or events from the past or anxieties about the future. Just note what they are, accept them and let them go. Remember, you are not trying to *suppress* thoughts but to let them go. That is your choice – either you can choose to follow them and become emotionally involved with the thoughts or you can choose to stand back a little and observe them simply as they float around in your mind. When you realise you are following thoughts, return your attention to your breath and let the thoughts go. You may feel you need to address some of the issues that are recurrent. If so, it may be helpful to use the wisdom of your inner self to guide you towards resolving the issues. Refer back to Section 1:13 The Higher Level Communication System if you need to remind yourself of the technique.

Practice this simple meditation every day and commit yourself to about six weeks practice and then you can assess the situation and notice the ways in which you have changed, whether it is how you feel physically, whether you are calmer emotionally and whether you are beginning to treat yourself more gently with compassion and understanding. Notice also whether you have become generally more alert and aware and observe any changes in the way you perceive your relationship with the world and the people in your life.

Bring to your practice an attitude of loving kindness towards yourself, this will grow and spread into a more compassionate view of others and the world. You will soon see the benefits from your meditation sessions and notice how the benefits overflow into enhancing your whole life as you learn to maintain your quiet centre of calmness.

11. Mantra Meditation

2

You may like to try the Mantra Meditation where your focus is the repetition of a meaningful word or words for the duration of the meditation period. For this we return to the idea of Bodymind Directions being given to the Bodymind Network to produce the desired effect. The Bodymind Directions for your mantra are:

'Peace' and 'Smile'.

These words are 'key words' which represent the longer Bodymind Directions as follows:

Key Word		Bodymind Direction
'Peace'	*represents*	**'Breathe in peace'**
'Smile'	*represents*	**'Breathe out and smile'**

Your mind has no difficulty in accepting each key word as a representation of the whole Bodymind Direction. Using 'peace' as a keyword will ensure your mind is focused upon the direction in which you want to move, that is, towards inner peace. The Bodymind Direction for peace will be passed on to your Bodymind Network which will respond accordingly. Using 'smile' as the other keyword will help you to maintain a sense of lightness about the meditation as well as creating feelings of happiness within you. Try the meditation as follows:

> Sit as before, comfortably, but in a position where you will still be alert. Make sure you are in a quiet place where you will be undisturbed for your chosen length of time (five minutes building up to fifteen or twenty as you progress). With your eyes closed and breathing through your nose, take your attention to your breath and just watch it as it gently flows in and out. Don't interfere with the pattern of your breathing and just let your body relax and quieten.

> Now, on your next in-breath, say to yourself, inside your head, 'Peace' and allow yourself to feel peaceful and calm.

> On the next out-breath say 'Smile' and as you relax with the out-breath allow yourself a gentle smile.

> Repeat these two in and out breaths for the chosen length of your meditation. Don't try to alter your breathing pattern to fit the words, just breathe naturally.

> If your attention wanders, as it will, gently return it to the focus of your breath and your mantra. As you continue with the meditation you will feel progressively more and more peaceful and serene.

If you wish, you could change the mantra words from 'peace' and 'smile' to a mantra of your own, perhaps 'love' or 'happiness'. On the other hand, some people prefer to use the word 'one' as a mantra as it has no emotional content. Others choose to count each out-breath for the duration of the meditation time, starting with one and going up to five and then beginning again. The choice is yours. You could try each different type of meditation, both mantra and breath awareness, just 'going with' each method to see what happens. Then practice the version of meditation with which you are most comfortable. The only really important factor is that you are actually practising; you can only benefit from whichever method you finally choose, as inner peace and serenity are the certain outcome of any form of meditation.

12. Sharing Your Inner Peace

Listening with Inner Peace

It is a wonderful thing to share your inner peace with others. When you are in a state of inner peace the effect spreads like ripples in water all around you in every direction, your inner peace touching all in its path. As it spreads, your peace will be returned back to you as the recipients of your peace begin to make ripples of their own.

You can transform your relationships with others using the practice of 'staying with the breath'. This method will allow you to share your own inner peace with the person you are speaking to, transforming and bringing alive your affinity with them.

When speaking with other people it's only too easy to be distracted and to have half a mind on their words, the rest of your attention on other matters; perhaps on the self, possibly thinking about the impression you are making; on what you are going to say next; on the time; on the weather; or on something you have to remember to do. The result of this diffused attention is reflected in the quality of your relationship with that person. They may even view you as being unfriendly, not interested in them or not sympathetic to their needs as they sense you are not fully involved with them.

> To be a satisfying and pleasing listener, give the person who is speaking the honour and dignity of your full attention. Do this no matter how rushed or busy you may be and regardless of any judgemental opinion of them you may currently hold. Look in their eyes, without staring, really focusing on what they are saying. Look at them with interest and listen to every word they are saying, really 'be there' for them. By listening in this way, they will think you are the most wonderful listener and that they are fascinating speakers. You will benefit also because by fixing yourself firmly in the present you reduce stress and enter a peaceful world that is close to a meditation.

As you listen, incorporate an awareness of your breath, allowing
it to be peaceful and calm. Really listen to the other person,
giving them your undivided attention but being at the same time
ever mindful of your breath in the way you would have an ear
half-cocked for a small child you were baby-sitting.

When you breathe consciously and with awareness you are firmly rooted
in the present and you become fully alive and a real person again. You
can then be totally with the person who is speaking and they also
become real and alive to you. You are also a more compassionate and
responsive listener, with anything you say being well thought out and
spoken in a calm, low-key voice. You can speak your truth and be open
and completely natural with them. You can look deeply at the other
person and so come to understand what they are really saying and what
their needs are. When you hear what they have to say you become filled
with compassion and feelings of loving kindness are extended towards
them. A real conversation with genuine meaning and feeling can now
take place. Your inner peace is spreading to encompass and surround
them and then, wonderfully, it becomes reflected back to you, so
enhancing and enriching your own being.

13. Inner Peace and Your Relationships

Understanding, Not Blaming

In the last exercise we talked of how your listening to others is filled
with a sense of compassion and understanding when you have an
awareness of your breath and feel centred in your inner peace. You can
use this knowledge to foster peace and calm in many areas of your life
where relationships are concerned.

From time to time you will come full tilt against the negative
emotions and actions of others as you mix with your family, friends,
those at work and with people at large. The negative emotional fall out
may be that you feel mocked, scorned, bullied or think you are treated
in some other displeasing way. When you come up against a problem like
this, the tendency is to blame the other person for causing the ill-will or
undesirable event in your life. Blaming does no good whatsoever. It is a

totally unproductive act which will not lead to an issue being resolved happily for either party. Both sides will continue to feel dissatisfied and unhappy and the status quo can never be re-established.

There is a different perspective you can take on this kind of situation and a way which is more in harmony with fostering your inner peace and tranquillity. Nhich Nhat Hanh, a famous Buddhist master, has much to say on how you can encourage relationships to blossom. His ideas are thus: if, when you plant a packet of lettuce seeds they don't shoot or grow well, you don't shout at the lettuce or blame it for not growing successfully. You know that blaming the lettuce is a fruitless exercise and will do nothing to make the plants grow more robustly. You look instead to find the reason why they have not thrived. You seek to understand. It is the same with people. Instead of blaming them, try to understand why they are acting the way they do. When you look into understanding why the other person has acted in a particular way you are taking full responsibility for the way you feel and for your reactions to the other person. Taking responsibility puts you in a position of personal power, from where you have a choice of action. When you understand the reasons for others' actions you are in a position to forgive and not blame.

If your partner is grouchy in the morning, it would be easy to snarl back but if, instead, you remember you heard your partner get up in the night and pace about, you would then be more understanding and more inclined towards compassion rather than irritation. You would ask if there was any way you could help, perhaps by either listening to what was the problem or by sharing some task to relieve the strain. Your partner would then see your sympathetic and kindly intent and begin to respond to your peace by replying in a quieter more loving way. Love and understanding go hand-in-hand. With understanding, your relationship with your partner will flourish. Harmony will be restored in a positive, compassionate and fruitful manner.

When you view others with compassion you are in a state of loving and in this state you cannot help but act in a way that will relieve their suffering. This way of approaching confrontation is extraordinarily self-nourishing, not only do you counter difficult situations and prevent them from escalating into far more damaging confrontations but, because you are in control of your thinking and your actions, your inner strengths of wisdom, self esteem and peace grow and flourish tenfold.

Healing Relationships

Sometimes you need to look a little deeper into understanding why someone has acted in a particular way. Remember that someone who is aggressive towards you in some way is also suffering; their aggression describes the state of *their* inner self, not yours. The negative emotion in the air is not your emotion, it is theirs and it is your choice whether or not you become affected by it. When you realise this, you realise you do not have to react in an aggressive manner yourself, a reaction which will get you nowhere productive or positive and can only harm both of you.

The other person's difficulties may have come about because of their mother or father's lack of skill as parents. This lack of skill may be traced back to their own parents and so on back through one generation after another. However, understanding and compassion have the power to overcome this negative repeat pattern and to break the cycle.

Once you can see the other person as a casualty of their upbringing and know that they are suffering too, you will have more understanding as to why they have acted in the way they have. With this understanding comes forgiveness and freedom from emotional pain. You lose your sense of blame and resentment and for you the problem is resolved, you can walk again with a light heart. As you deal with the person with compassion and loving kindness the peace that flows from you will be perceived by the other person and the healing process can begin.

Some people get 'stuck' with an attitude of blame all their lives, perhaps blaming their father, mother, partner or even 'fate' or 'the stars' for their current difficulties. But the need to blame your parents or anything else disappears and you become free from blame and from repeating the patterns of the past by taking responsibility for your own self and your own emotions. You do this when you live with peace in your heart and look with eyes of understanding and compassion at what happened to you when you were a child, or what has happened to make the other person suffer. In the case of your own early upbringing, remember that you are a new and different person who is operating now from love and peace and not from an irrational, thoughtless repeated pattern from the past. With this awareness you know you have choice, the choice to live with inner peace in your heart, being motivated not by blame but by compassion. As for 'fate' and 'the stars', remember that you have free will and can make your own decisions and choices in life. Knowing you have choice will always make you feel more in control, more powerful. Always be aware of the many choices you have in actions and feelings. Choose that which makes you peaceful.

The process for healing holds true even if the other person is not present at the time. They don't need to be there for the healing to begin. Healing starts with the self and flows outwards to others. Heal yourself by treating yourself with compassion and understanding and then you will find this regard extends to others in the same way. Forgiveness, reconciliation and acceptance follow. Inner peace and harmony prevail.

Forgiveness

People often say, 'I can see why someone did that but I'll never forgive them.' If you don't want to or don't know how to forgive you will never forget and will continue to harbour resentment and other negative emotions which can only be harmful to you. You will have a sense of separation from yourself and from really loving yourself. You will feel 'prickly', edgy or irritable and deep down inside yourself lonely and isolated.

The act of forgiveness allows you to release these negative emotions and come into inner balance and peace. *You* will be the principal beneficiary from forgiveness as all the hurt from the past will be healed, erased and forgotten, you will be free from the past. Forgiveness, like compassion, understanding and loving, begins with the self. Once you have forgiven yourself for whatever it may be, you are able to forgive others. Your sense of love, both towards yourself and to others is free to be restored.

When you forgive, you become free from trying to control events and circumstances – happenings over which you can never have control anyway. An attitude of forgiveness gives you freedom as you learn to stop judging yourself to be different from how you are and to accept yourself as you are. This approach leaves you free to stop judging others, and to accept them also as they are.

Forgiveness is an act of letting go, it does not imply a liking or condoning of the person or act involved. Even if you feel you have been unjustly treated in some way or have done something yourself that you now judge is something to be ashamed of, sorry for or guilty about. It does you no good to hang on to those feelings of bitterness, guilt or blame. If the negative feelings are directed towards someone else you are hurting yourself more than you are hurting the other person. If the negative feelings are directed towards yourself there is no positive purpose to it – why hurt yourself like this when you can be free of the pain?

If you are harbouring feelings of guilt about events or actions in the past it is time to realise that guilt is a completely useless emotion. You are making judgements about yourself with your *current* knowledge, not the knowledge you had at that time. With hindsight we can all see alternative ways we could have chosen to behave but at the time of the incident, whatever it was, we acted in the only way we knew how. If we had known another way at the time, we would have chosen that way.

You need to forgive yourself when you are feeling not good enough in some way. Know instead that you are good enough just as you are, always have been and always will be – recognise and acknowledge this and let go of judgemental views about yourself and others. You can do no more than you know how to and neither can anyone else. This is not an excuse for complacency, we all grow and change as life moves on, developing and learning from our past mistakes and experiences. But why choose the path that makes you suffer when you can choose the path of inner peace and happiness?

So, be gentle with yourself, let go of the past, forgive yourself for judging and criticising both yourself and others. By letting go of resentment, guilt and blame you allow the past to stay where it belongs, leaving you free to live your life in the present and able to move on.

To forgive, all you need is to be *willing* to forgive, willing to release yourself from the uncomfortable or distressing feelings. To forgive you need to acknowledge that you no longer wish to bear a grudge or to be judgemental about either yourself or another person. Use the exercise that follows to release yourself from any unwanted feelings.

Self-forgiveness Exercise

Try this exercise which is aimed at either self-forgiveness or forgiving others.

For this exercise you need to be in a place where you can be quiet and undisturbed for a while, perhaps 5 – 15 minutes. Before you do the exercise it is a good idea to complete the Tune-in Session and the Tune-in Bodymind Directions as in Section 1 and then continue with the self-forgiveness exercise as follows:

Sit quietly or even lie down and let yourself get very peaceful and comfortable.

Shut your eyes, relax and be still............

Imagine you are totally surrounded by a protective white light. Feel very calm and at one with yourself. Allow your breath to become a little slower, a little deeper and really feel peace spreading through you.

Now imagine that you are sitting in front of a big television screen. There are two buttons on the set. Reach out and switch the set on with the left hand button. The picture that comes on the screen is of a yacht, far out at sea near the horizon. It is a peaceful scene. The sky is a pale blue and the sea is a calm greeny-blue colour. The yacht has large white sails which are filled with the light afternoon breeze. On the sails there is **'forgive'** written in large gold letters...........

When you are ready, ask your Inner Wisdom,

'Who or what is it I need to forgive?

The answer may come as a thought, a word, a picture or a sensation of some sort. Go gently and take your time.........

Now see the people involved or the situation itself as being small enough to put in the yacht. Notice how seeing the picture on the set distances you from the action. You feel perfectly safe and secure.

With understanding, compassion and a desire to forgive, say to them,

> **'I am willing to forgive** ....(myself/other person)
> **for**....................' (Complete as appropriate)

Now, press the button on the right and as you do so the yacht will gradually sail over the horizon and out of sight.

All you can see now are the white sails with 'forgive' written in gold letters. As the yacht slowly sails away, the word 'forgive' very gradually begins to sink down over the horizon. As you watch, hold your hands, palm up, out in front of you in a gesture of letting go. Give the Bodymind Direction,

> **'Let the past go'**....................
> (PAUSE AND WAIT, NOTICE THE RESPONSE)

Really feel the lightness as the burden from the past floats away from you. The word 'forgive' is disappearing right over the horizon and as it disappears you feel lighter and lighter.

Now give these extra Bodymind Directions:

> **Know now that the past is over and done with.**
> (PAUSE AND WAIT, NOTICE ANY RESPONSE)

> **Forgive and let go all that is not love.**
> (PAUSE AND WAIT, NOTICE ANY RESPONSE)

> **Let harmony and peace fill your life.**
> (PAUSE AND WAIT, NOTICE ANY RESPONSE)

You are now free, free from the episode in the past.

2

Now feel the white light that surrounds you permeate into your body, cleansing, purifying and refreshing you. Feel completely free from the past, light and joyful.

Very slowly and gently bring yourself back to your room, feeling the peace and freedom within you.

You can do this exercise as many times as you need until you feel completely cleansed and free from the past. You will know you are making progress by the strength of the sense of lightness you feel afterwards.

In the future, if you find you are being self-critical in any way or filled with guilt, blame or resentment, be sure to use the exercise again to counter the emotion. Foster this attitude of forgiveness as you continue through life so that you are never 'stuck' with guilt, blame or other negative emotions.

14. Bodymind Directions for Inner Peace

Remember to use the Tuning-In session first to still your body and mind. See Section 1 if you need to remind yourself of the process.

Tune-in Bodymind Directions

Say the Tune-in Bodymind Directions aloud or just under your breath with a clear, gentle but firm voice. **Take your time.** Leave a pause of at least half a minute between each Tune-in Bodymind Direction. Remember you can intensify any response by saying 'more and more' or 'faster than this', or similar phrases of your own as appropriate.

1. **Feel calm and confident.**
(PAUSE AND WAIT, NOTICE ANY RESPONSE)

2. **Smile and feel happy.**
(PAUSE AND WAIT, NOTICE ANY RESPONSE)

3. Release anything negative from your body, mind and spirit.
(PAUSE AND WAIT, NOTICE ANY RESPONSE)

4. Fill your entire being with loving kindness towards yourself and the world.
(PAUSE AND WAIT, NOTICE ANY RESPONSE)

5. Feel full of vibrant health and energy. Sparkle with confidence. Glow with joy.
(PAUSE AND WAIT, NOTICE ANY RESPONSE)

Bodymind Directions for Inner Peace
Select two or three of the following Bodymind Directions that you feel are appropriate for you at this moment:

1. Breathe in and SMILE.
(PAUSE AND WAIT, NOTICE ANY RESPONSE)

2. Breathe out and feel peaceful and calm.
(PAUSE AND WAIT, NOTICE ANY RESPONSE)

3. You are filled with inner peace.
(PAUSE AND WAIT, NOTICE ANY RESPONSE)

4. Let the peace spread to all around you.
(PAUSE AND WAIT, NOTICE ANY RESPONSE)

5. Let your relationships be bound by understanding and compassion.
(PAUSE AND WAIT, NOTICE ANY RESPONSE)

6. Let your peace be felt in all you do and say.
(PAUSE AND WAIT, NOTICE ANY RESPONSE)

7. Release anything that is not love in your life..
(PAUSE AND WAIT, NOTICE ANY RESPONSE)

8. **Forgive and let go all that is not love in your life.**
(PAUSE AND WAIT, NOTICE ANY RESPONSE)

9. **Know that the past is over and done with.**
(PAUSE AND WAIT, NOTICE ANY RESPONSE)

10. **Let harmony and peace fill your life.**
(PAUSE AND WAIT, NOTICE ANY RESPONSE)

15. Review

1. Inner peace and happiness are in the here and now, not at some time in the future when you have achieved or obtained something.

2. Build the 'Breathe and Smile Mantra' into your day (2:3).

3. For a real treat give yourself a 'smile bath' with the 'Body Smiling' exercise (5).

4. Every evening 'Maximise your Inner Peace and Happiness' (6).

5. Practice the simple 'Meditation for Inner Peace' (10).

6. Practice the Mantra Meditation in one of its forms (11).

7. Develop your Listening Skills to build constructive, loving relationships (12).

8. Foster an attitude of understanding and forgiveness towards confrontational situations (3).

9. Use the Bodymind Directions for Inner Peace (14).

None of these ideas take much time out of your busy day and taking even one of them on board will transform your life so begin that process right here and **START NOW**.

How to feel peaceful right NOW, this moment.

Look up from the book, take a deep breath and breathe in peace. **Enjoy** this moment: give the Bodymind Directions, 'Breathe in peace.......... breathe out peace to the wider world'. Then take a few moments to appreciate your surroundings, the sky, whatever its mood; to smell the roses; appreciate the trees and the grass; the view out of the window, whatever it is. Use this simple but powerful technique many times throughout the day.

2

Feel good about yourself

1. The Path to Feeling Good About Yourself

When you feel good about yourself you act with confidence and enjoy high self-esteem, you feel at one with yourself and generally feel content with who you are. You enjoy feelings of vitality and have sufficient energy for all you want to do, you feel joyful and full of gratitude for all you have and indeed for life itself. When you feel good about yourself it becomes easy to focus on the good in life and to appreciate the world around you and everything you touch appears to happen effortlessly and without a struggle; life flows.

Happiness comes from feeling good about yourself and accepting yourself as you are, just as you are right now. Without trying to *prove* anything to anyone, without trying to *be* anything for anyone. Just being *yourself* is good enough. We all thrive and grow in an atmosphere of approval and praise. This applies to us as adults as well as when we were children. When we don't feel we are good enough we may find our lives run by feelings of anger, fear or guilt. As adults, we can provide a nurturing atmosphere of love, acceptance and peace for ourselves – and who better than ourselves to provide it? We know ourselves better than anyone else and so know exactly where congratulation and appreciation are due. You are a remarkable person with your own unique abilities, qualities and skills. You are special and deserve happiness, just because you are *you*. If you focus on *deserving* to have what you want, that's what your experience will be. When you tell yourself that you are worthy of abundant happiness, this will be your reality.

Much of what is called happiness originates in the way you view your life, your environment and the events within them. This view stems from the way you think about yourself and the outside world. Many of us are in captivity to our feelings, feelings that can swing from anger, to love, to anxiety or fear, to euphoria. Your feelings, including happiness, stem from the thoughts you think. Every thought you think resonates at cellular level creating either a positive or negative effect on your whole being. Your thoughts are powerful. Indeed, you are what you *think* you are. Your happiness and even your health are often a direct reflection of the messages you are giving to yourself. You truly can 'think yourself happy' and 'think yourself healthy'. The trick to creating the life you want is to *believe* you deserve and can achieve that life. This transformation can be assured with the support of your Inner Wisdom.

When you are 'off the happiness path' and out of balance, calm, logical thought and the ability to relax and keep matters in perspective disappears. In this section you will discover how you can use your inner powers to sweep away negative, unhelpful thoughts which bring you down. You will be shown how to focus on those thoughts that will nourish your emotional health by fostering the sense of happiness and well being which will allow you to feel increasingly good about yourself. It will also be revealed to you how to deal with challenging situations so that rather than being a force for distress, they become a teacher for you allowing you to return to your centre of peace with even greater inner strength.

You will discover that, although you can't always change what is happening to you, you *can* learn to change the way you *think* about events and be more in control of the way you want to feel. In addition, you will become even further attuned to your inner life, something we often neglect. When you become in touch with and develop your inner life, with its deep core of wisdom and truth, you free up your creative abilities and give yourself the opportunity to become a more positive, energised joyful person, able to cope with daily stresses and strains. You become invigorated and ready to embrace whatever comes your way to the full, learning how to feel good about yourself and walk the path through life you wish to walk. Moreover, you will learn how to make the time in your busy day for these beneficial changes to take place.

Read the first part of this section and then go on to read the second part, which divulges how, through the unique Bodymind Directions, you can feel good about your body, promote sparkling vital health and overcome pain and other ailments.

PART ONE - *Happy Thoughts Make a Happy Life*

2. Automatic Bodymind Directions

It was a revelation to me when, many years ago, I first became truly aware of the many thoughts that entered my mind. I was astonished at some of the negative instructions I was giving myself at an automatic, almost below consciousness, level.

As I discovered, normally we are not fully mindful of all the many and different types of thoughts that pass through our heads. Throughout the day your mind produces thousands of thoughts, some with a neutral slant, some positive, but most of us spend our lives governed by a stream of negative, self-defeating thoughts, in sentence or word form. These thoughts seem to come from nowhere, they don't appear to be within our control and it's almost as though there is another person in there whose function it is to criticize, censure and cast doubt upon everything we do or say. This 'inner critic' often keeps us on 'red alert' in a state of tension and anxiety, with our thoughts reduced to short tabloid-type headlines, such as 'Can't do it', 'Fail', 'That's rubbish', or 'It won't work', 'Not good enough' or 'Must do that *NOW*', which then cascade like an unceasing waterfall at the back of our mind.

These negative thoughts from your 'inner critic' have been laid down over the years, probably since childhood. However, you weren't born with negative thoughts running through your mind, they arose as a result of your experiences in life. As children, we are normally trained to behave in an acceptable manner by constant, well-intentioned, repetition of phrases such as 'Don't do that', 'Don't touch', 'That's bad', 'You can't do that', all of which tend to make us cautious and lacking in confidence and joy.

With repetition over the years these phrases, or similar ones, are produced automatically from somewhere deep in our minds. Because we have been listening to them for so long, we subconsciously *believe* these negative thoughts and so set ourselves up to fail, be anxious, feel pressurized and generally be off the golden path of happiness. These automatic negative thoughts are just like the positive Bodymind Directions you have been using in previous sections in that they affect your body and mind. Observe the hold they can have on you and what negative effects they can have. With their constant repetition over a lifetime you can see just how successful Bodymind Directions are!

Until it is pointed out to us, we don't always realise that we have this incessant stream of negative thoughts and we certainly don't appreciate how they affect us. It is good to be aware of these adverse or negative thoughts so that you can come to understand and deal with them.

If you think back to Feel-good Factor 1 you will remember the 'pencil' exercise which showed you quite dramatically just how powerful are your thoughts. If you would like to remind yourself of that exercise go back right now to page 13 and try it again.

As you discovered in the 'pencil' experiment, negative thoughts, or Negative Bodymind Directions, weaken your muscular response, but positive thoughts, or Positive Bodymind Directions, strengthen your reaction. Although you only noticed the different responses in your fingers, the physical reaction will not only have taken place in your hands, of course, but throughout your whole body, weakening or strengthening it according to the type of thoughts you introduced.

The outcome of the experiment has far-reaching implications for you. If negative thoughts of just a few seconds duration can weaken your response so much, just think what continuous anxiety, unhappiness and other negative conditions are capable of doing to your body and the way in which it functions. To back your own findings, the medical profession has now produced conclusive scientific evidence to show irrefutably that thoughts directly affect the function of the body at basic cellular level. As soon as a thought enters your mind it is translated immediately into physical or emotional reality, as instantly as switching on a light.

The exciting news for you is that much of what has ever been written about positive thinking really is valid – you really cannot afford the luxury of a negative thought and you truly can have a positive input into your own health and happiness.

When you are in a positive frame of mind with a positive attitude towards life you will feel confident, vibrant, lively and happy, you will feel in control of your life. With a positive approach to life we not only feel good emotionally but another benefit is that you can actually improve your physical health. The positive vibrations running through you extend to releasing your body's own self-healing mechanisms including endorphins, the agent that essentially promotes that wonderful relaxed and 'feel-good' sensation you enjoy when you are in an upbeat mood.

As I have mentioned before, you thrive and grow in a climate of praise, support and love. Once an adult, *you* take the responsibility of providing this loving atmosphere and environment for *yourself*. Although you may have had a lifetime to practise giving yourself Negative Bodymind Directions, it does not mean it is too late to change direction now. You are about to discover how to overcome any long term negative tendency and replace it with a positive, optimistic outlook on life.

3. The Power in Your Mind

You can overcome any long term negative tendency and replace it with a positive and optimistic outlook on life because **you** are the Power in your mind, so you can choose to think the thoughts that are personally nourishing and supportive. As you know, your mind produces thoughts all day long, thoughts of every kind and colour. It is perfectly normal and acceptable to have negative thoughts about any situation or event in your life, difficulties only arise when you actually *believe* your negative thoughts. Yes, just because your *think* a thought, it doesn't mean it is *true*. You are more than your thoughts. You are the Consciousness, the Power *behind* the thoughts, the 'Power in your Mind'. Although you have no control over which thoughts come to your mind, you are the Power in your mind, not the thought. Having this dominance means that you can be selective with your thoughts. You, as the 'Thinker behind the Thoughts' have the choice at any moment to either dismiss a thought or to take it on board.

Once you realise that automatic thoughts have the same power to affect your body as Bodymind Directions, the knowledge that you can *choose* what you think is extraordinarily empowering. Being fully aware of the consequences of believing your negative thoughts and the effect they have on your body, you can choose whether to go along with a negative thought or whether to let it go as being inappropriate and no longer valid for you. You also have the ability and authority to deliberately introduce new thoughts of your own, thoughts that are supporting and upbeat to fill you with energy and vitality.

> To understand fully what it means to be the 'Power in your Mind', imagine for a moment that all the thoughts you think in a day are like the TV listings for the day. When it comes to planning your viewing, although there are hundreds of programmes printed out for you, you appreciate that you can't watch everything. You, having control of the TV 'zapper', scan the programmes for items that appeal to you. In fact, you don't even have to choose any of the programmes at all if you don't like what is on offer. Having the 'Power of the Zapper', you can choose **NOT** to watch the television that day.

> Thoughts are the same, thousands of thoughts run through your mind every day but you, as the 'Power in your Mind', don't have to take note of any of them if you don't want to, you can choose to let them go.

> Going back to the idea of selecting television programmes again, you can even choose not to watch any of the listed programmes, but to watch a video of your own choice instead. Again, this is exactly the same with thoughts. You can introduce new, different thoughts of your own, to replace the thoughts you don't want. **You are the Thinker in your mind.**

The importance of recognizing that *you* are the Power in your Mind cannot be stressed too much. As I mentioned before, you cannot choose the thoughts that enter your head but you do have the choice always of selecting which of those thoughts to either follow or let go. For example, as you read this page, you may be aware of occasional thoughts intruding, perhaps thoughts such as wondering what you are having for your next meal, thoughts about your next commitment, thoughts about your comfort, or thoughts about your friends or family. Because you are otherwise occupied in reading at the moment you appreciate that these thoughts can wait and so you let them go, knowing you can pick up on them later if you wish.

You will not always be really aware of all the types of thoughts that arise like bubbles in your mind, but some of those that reach your consciousness may have a positive slant, some may be slightly negative or anxious and some may be neutral. This is perfectly normal, we all perceive a whole variety of different types of thoughts. No thought is inherently either 'bad' or 'good', it is just a thought. What you do about a thought and how you label each one is up to you. And so, developing a positive attitude does not mean that you will never think another 'negative' thought, it just means that you will learn how to dismiss those thoughts that are of an undermining nature and seek out and concentrate upon thoughts that are more supportive and promote happiness and enjoyment in your life.

4. Interpretation of Situations

It really is possible to nurture and develop a cheerful, positive attitude to life. There's no doubt that with this change in attitude you will certainly feel good about yourself. As with thoughts, no situation in itself is 'bad' or 'good', a situation is just a situation. It is your attitude towards the situation and your interpretation of the situation that colours it as being either 'bad' or 'good' or neither.

Circumstances themselves may not be open to change but the way you choose to view them can be changed.

All situations can be viewed in two ways. The significance of any event or incident is in what you think about it, your attitude towards it and your interpretation of it. Instead of looking for frightening, anger-provoking, censuring or other elements within an occurrence you can choose instead to seek positive aspects or choose to place your attention elsewhere towards different and more rewarding matters.

REMEMBER ALWAYS –
'Being positive' means **focusing** on the positive.

'Being positive' means you will become more aware of your thoughts and learn how to handle them, changing them to more life-enhancing thoughts. Remember that in the interest of your health, both physical and emotional, it is not desirable to let unhappy thoughts roost in your mind. Change your thoughts and you can change your attitude and the way your body functions. No matter for how long you have been less than truly happy it is always possible to change and learn to have some awareness of and control over your thoughts. Learning this skill is an essential ingredient in the 'happiness process'.

To dismiss anxious, stressful thoughts may seem a challenging task but you are already well practised in letting unwanted thoughts go. Returning to the discussion about the thoughts that arose whilst you were reading, you knew without thinking about it, how to let go of the thoughts that you didn't want to follow up at that time. You did this by deliberately bringing your attention back to what you were doing, that is, reading. You can learn to do exactly the same with any joyless thought that arises, letting it go, over and over again, if necessary. With the technique that I will explain later on you can learn how to stop these unwanted automatic Negative Bodymind Directions or thoughts in their tracks and introduce in their place thoughts that are optimistic and joyful.

5. Define Your Automatic Negative Bodymind Directions/Thoughts

Firstly, you can't dismiss your Negative Bodymind Directions unless you can recognize them for what they are. Remember, these are *automatic* negative thoughts that we think so habitually we are hardly aware of them. So, it is necessary to begin with becoming more aware of just what you are thinking in order to catch the automatic thoughts. To do this you need to start *listening* to your thoughts and thought patterns. Sometimes it is even difficult to decide precisely whether a thought is negative or not. For instance, even unthinking swearing such as, 'Oh damn it', or worse, when the phone rings can be classed as negative inner talk! A negative thought is one which is blocking, restricting, limiting, self-defeating, one which is not constructive, which is less than welcoming and neither upbeat nor joyful. Be particularly aware of thoughts which begin with or contain words such as:

'must'

'ought'

'should'

'never'

'always'.

Whether they refer to yourself or someone else these words are extremely restricting and inhibiting. Cast them out of your vocabulary and in their place use words such as:

'I may.....'

'I choose to.....'

'They might......'

'Sometimes I.....'

This choice of word allows for some freedom and openness and they are more likely to lead you towards the 'happiness response' in your body and mind.

    These are some further examples of negative/positive thought and speech patterns for you to look out for:

Joyless, Limiting Attitude	Life-enhancing, Creative Attitude
'I've got to ......'	'I may.....'
'I must......'	'I choose to.....'
'I should.....'	'I could.....'
'I ought.....'	'I might.....'
'What if .....'	'It's not really likely that .....'
'How can I cope?'	'I know how to handle this.....'
'It's awful.....'	'It's a learning experience......'
'I'll never get/be......'	'I will .....'
'She always does ......'	'Sometimes she ......'

Remember that every moment is a fresh start for you and an opportunity to choose the 'happiness path' with a life-enhancing attitude, or to choose otherwise. You always have this choice and it is never too late to begin. Each time you deliberately choose the 'happiness path' and use life-enhancing thoughts or speech it makes it easier to travel upon that path again in the future. You are making new habits, new pathways for yourself and the more you use them, the more marked the tracks become and the easier to follow, just like making tracks through the undergrowth in a wood or through the long grass in a field. Over time you will notice that your automatic thought patterns are changing. Your thoughts will be more supportive and uplifting and they will allow for more creative possibilities within your life. For example, which of these two thought patterns is the more creative and with which are you more likely to succeed?

'I'll never be able to ....' (insert your own fear)

or

'This is a real challenge for me but I'll give it my best shot.'

3

Gradually it will become second-nature for you to seek out and use positive, life-enhancing inner talk and your automatic negative thoughts and consequently Negative Bodymind Directions will lessen. When you've learnt how to replace the negative aspect of your inner dialogue with optimistic, self-supporting and mood-raising inner talk, your happiness is assured. Meanwhile, when you notice you are using limiting inner talk, instead of using it as an occasion to criticize yourself, use it instead as an opportunity to bestow compassion and understanding upon yourself and congratulate yourself for noticing the difference between self-defeating thoughts and life-enhancing thoughts. Remember, we tend to wither and decline in a restrictive and critical atmosphere, whereas we thrive and blossom in a climate of love and empathy, so let that be your natural way of being.

Now you can find out what are your own personal type of limiting thoughts. The following exercise will help you to become aware of some of the thoughts you habitually think.

6. Catch Your Automatic Negative Bodymind Directions

This activity will be an illuminating experience for you. So make yourself comfortable in a place where you will be undisturbed for about a quarter of an hour. You will need two pieces of paper and a pen or pencil for this exercise.

1. Write the heading 'Statements About Myself' on one of the pieces of paper, and then write down any **one** of the following short statements. Choose one that has particular resonance for you, one you would like to think was authentic for you even if it doesn't ring true at the moment:

I love and approve of myself.
I am happy and joyful.
I am full of health and vitality.
I accept myself just as I am.
I am safe and secure and all is well.
I give love out and love returns to me.
I am successful in all I do.
I am full of confidence.

You are going to write your chosen statement over and over on the sheet of paper headed 'Statements About Myself'. Each time you complete the sentence, pause, and just allow thoughts to come to your mind spontaneously in response to the sentiment in the statement. Don't **try** to think, let thoughts appear by themselves. Above all, don't be judgemental about the contents of the thoughts. This exercise is for your eyes only and merely to help you to become aware of your thoughts.

Write the heading 'Automatic Negative Bodymind Directions' on your second piece of paper, and on this sheet, you will write down each thought as it arises in response to the chosen statement about yourself, **no matter what it is**. Make sure you write them all down.

2. Begin now, by writing your statement on the first piece of paper, then note down the thoughts that arise in response to it on the second piece of paper.

When no more thoughts arise, write your original statement again on your first piece of paper. As before, pause and allow time for further thoughts to arise in response. Write them down once more on your second sheet of paper.

Continue in this way, writing first your statement, pausing to allow thoughts to arise and then writing the thoughts that emerge as a response. Do this until you have written the original statement twenty times.

Towards the end of writing the statement you may well discover that, in reply to the statement, no more thoughts are surfacing in your consciousness. However, don't stop, keep on writing your statement until you have written it twenty times in all. Writing it will serve to impress the desired sentiment upon your subconscious mind and will be a first step towards the realisation in your life of the idea within the statement.

Remember, there are no 'right or wrong' responses in this exercise. The exercise is merely to raise your awareness about the type of thoughts you think.

In writing the statement you will not only allow negative thoughts to arise to consciousness but, in doing so, you will be easing their grip, a first step in eliminating your Automatic Negative Bodymind Directions.

When you have completed the exercise, quickly scan the page with your written responses to your statement in order to identify your own personal limiting beliefs. You will find that these words, phrases or sentences probably crop up regularly in your thoughts. You will possibly recognise from where the thoughts originated, but don't spend any time thinking about it, it doesn't matter. Once you have scanned the list – *THROW IT AWAY* without reading it again. Re-reading would only serve to reinforce the very ideas you have just released.

Now, take your statement and use it as a Positive Bodymind Direction. This is the list of 'Statements About Myself' transformed into Positive Bodymind Directions:

You love and approve of yourself.
Feel happy and joyful.
Feel full of health and vitality.
Accept yourself just as you are.
Feel safe and secure and know that all is well.
You give love out and so find love returning to you.
You're successful in all you do.
You sparkle with confidence.

Read your Positive Bodymind Directions out aloud to yourself and repeat them again and again, leaving a pause between each repetition so that the full effect may have time to be realized. Even more effective is to look at yourself in a mirror and repeat the Bodymind Direction wholeheartedly and with real feeling, over and over to yourself in the mirror until you feel it working for you. Do this exercise every day for best results.

You can continue to use this exercise on a daily basis using any uplifting Positive Bodymind Directions of your choice. Repetition of your chosen Positive Bodymind Directions will bring the sentiments within it to reality.

Use the whole process to explore any negative feelings you may have about any particular area of your life. The process will dissolve those negative mental blocks and release you into freedom of thought and action.

Catch Your Automatic Negative Bodymind Directions Throughout the Day

This is a good exercise to help you discover just what Automatic Negative Bodymind Directions you are giving yourself throughout the day.

Set your watch or a timer for half an hour and then continue with your day as normal. When the bell rings, make a note of your thoughts at the time, whatever they are. Repeat this exercise throughout your day or for part of the day.

When you have collected a page or so of thoughts examine your list. Are they biased towards being life-enhancing or limiting statements, positive or negative Bodymind Directions? Were there many critical thoughts either of yourself or of others? Were the thoughts about the past or the future?

As before, there are no 'right or wrong' answers. This exercise is merely to raise your awareness about the type of thoughts you think. Don't spend any time trying to analyse the thoughts. After scanning them briefly, **THROW THE PAPER AWAY** and treat yourself to some life-affirming statements from the list in this section.

7. Challenging Your Automatic Negative Bodymind Directions

After completing these exercises you will have become familiar with some of your personal Automatic Negative Bodymind Directions. Remember, we **ALL** have a tendency to produce Automatic Negative Bodymind Directions, what you need to know now is how to **deal** with them once you have found them.

Sometimes you may find you are following a whole train of thoughts, one Automatic Negative Bodymind Direction leading to another. When you become aware of this happening, challenge the Automatic Negative Bodymind Direction with this question:

'Are these thoughts really TRUE?'

You will find when you respond to your limiting thoughts with this question and give yourself a rational answer that the thoughts generally are not true, certainly not 100% true. If, for example, you were thinking along the lines again of 'You'll never get this finished.....', when you look back later in the day, were you right, partly right, or did you, in fact, achieve what you were doing?

When you realise that on the whole your Automatic Negative

Bodymind Directions are not correct, not to be trusted and are giving you out of date information, you will gain much confidence. Henry Ford always said, *'If you think you can, you can, if you think you can't, you're right.'* In other words, *'You are what you think you are'*. If you continually think you are late/no good/inadequate/can't finish the task/unhappy, that is what your experience will be. However, as the 'Power in your Mind' and having the power to think whatever thoughts you wish, if you tell yourself instead that you have plenty of time/are totally adequate at all times/are successful and happy, then *this* will be your reality.

Remember – what you *think* will ultimately result in how you *feel*.

8. Eliminating Your Automatic Negative Bodymind Directions

Each and every second is a new opportunity for change. When you accept that each moment in time is a new starting point, a choice point, where you can opt either to go along with a thought or to dismiss it, you have the power to transform your life. The key to achieving this transformation is the knowledge of how to arrest your mental flow of negative statements, thus transforming your inner voice into a friend. When you become aware of Automatic Negative Bodymind Directions racing through your mind eliminate them like this:

At the very first moment you notice you are thinking negatively or giving yourself Automatic Negative Bodymind Directions, say to yourself in a firm, convincing voice, either out aloud or inside your head,

'STOP!'

When you first try this you will be amazed at the effect it has. At once there is an astounded silence in your mind as it registers the unexpected and sudden intervention. Your mind is, after all, used to being in total command, having its own way and producing whatever thoughts it pleases completely unchecked. Your mind can be very resistant and won't take kindly to being spoken to in this way, so, before it has the opportunity to start producing yet more negative thoughts, show it that you, the 'Power in your Mind', are back in charge and not about to give it any leeway. Quickly take advantage of that sudden lull in activity and fill the space with one of your upbeat, mood-raising statements which, of course, you will already have prepared just for that very purpose. Here is a selection to choose from.

A Selection of Positive, Life-enhancing Bodymind Directions

Use just one or two of the following uplifting Bodymind Directions that resonate with you at the time or if you prefer to make your own, see the instructions below:

> 'You are more and more positive in your body, mind and spirit every day.'
> 'It is EASY to......' (be joyful/complete this task/forgive your friend, etc).
> 'Be still. This will pass.' (A perfect Bodymind Direction for times of stress.)
> 'Feel calm and confident.'
> 'Your life is filled with joy.'
> 'Be happy and content.'
> 'Concentrate on the joyful aspects of your life.'
> 'Love and approve of yourself.'
> 'Accept yourself as you are.'
> 'Feel good about yourself.'
> 'Your self-esteem is high and you're filled with confidence.'
> 'Your entire being is filled with happiness NOW!'
> 'Feel stronger and stronger every day.'
> 'Feel more and more positive every day.'
> 'Be aware of and thankful for the good in your life.'
> 'Fill your entire being with loving kindness towards yourself and the world.'

Repeat your chosen statement or Positive Bodymind Direction over and over, out aloud or silently. Use a convincing, strong and clear tone of voice, whether aloud or in your head, until you feel confident that your feelings are coming into line with the statement. Pause after each repetition of your Bodymind Direction and leave time for the effect to be felt, either physically, mentally, emotionally or spiritually.

Now you are experienced in giving Bodymind Directions you may not necessarily need to go through the whole of the Tuning-in session, as described in Section 1. However, if you feel the Bodymind Directions you are giving are not taking full effect, take the time to go through the whole Tuning-in process. It is well worth the extra few minutes to do so.

It's best to select just one or two Bodymind Directions to use at a time or there will be too much information for your Bodymind Network to cope with. For maximum effect and to ensure that your mind is fed a new diet of uplifting thoughts to 're-programme' it, repeat your chosen Bodymind Directions as many times as you can throughout the day. You are training your mind by nudging it gently and persistently towards the positive. Some people like to write their Bodymind Directions on small cards to keep in a pocket or bag to read at quiet moments. Reading the Bodymind Directions makes it easier to recall them and reinforces the words in your Bodymind Network.

The wisdom behind your Bodymind Network is not selective or judgemental. Like a gullible child it takes on board anything you instruct it, whether true or false. This is wonderful knowledge, as it means that you can feed your subconscious mind with all the most generous and uplifting Bodymind Directions you can possibly imagine. Providing you say the Bodymind Directions in a wholehearted and convincing manner, your Bodymind Network won't disagree with you and will accept whatever you tell it. The ideas within the Bodymind Directions are then transmitted to your Bodymind Network which responds accordingly, bringing the ideas and your reality closer together.

Over time, you will notice that with continual use of the technique, your mindset will have changed in a subtle yet positive and welcome way. You will automatically be thinking in a more dynamic, optimistic and constructive way. You will be feeling happier and more contented in every respect as your Automatic Negative Bodymind Directions steadily dwindle away. You will have created Automatic Positive

Bodymind Directions in their place. This self-directing technique is central to the process of transforming your life. It is a means of feeling good about yourself at any given moment in your life. Never forget that you are what you *think* you are and so refuse to listen to those Automatic Negative Bodymind Directions and take advantage of the powerful 'STOP' technique to change to mood-raising, self-supporting Positive Bodymind Directions.

9. What Governs Your Life?

Whatever governs your life determines the shape of it. Consider what it is that governs *your* life at the moment. It may be work, your career, money, a relationship. When these things rule your life the paths they lead you along may not be in your best interests. Let your Inner Wisdom, your natural sense of goodness, your 'best self' govern your life and then everything you do will be for your good and your benefit. You will be truly and firmly on the happiness path and you will be taking others with you. When we radiate happiness, loving kindness and compassion, everyone benefits. And so let your inner goodness shine out and allow its love and joy to touch all who enter your presence.

All relationships need nurturing and the relationship with your inner self is no exception. We all thrive on praise and approval and so spend a few minutes every day giving this to yourself, your inner self. With encouragement and respect your inner being will flourish and this attention will repay you a thousandfold as the joy from within pours out and all around you and is reflected back to you – happiness indeed.

When your innate sense of goodness is the governing power in your life you will find *real* happiness. When you tune in to your inner life and voice, you free up your creative abilities and give yourself the opportunity to become a more positive, energised and joyful person, able to cope with your daily stresses and strains. Life flows, you become invigorated and ready to embrace life to the full – you truly do feel good about yourself.

PART TWO – *Feeling Good About Your Body*

10. Your Body Image

We would all like to feel good about our body, yet this is one area where there seems to be a blockage for some people, many of whom have a poor image of their body or aspects of it. This personal image bears no relationship to the reality of their body and the way it is actually perceived by other people. Your body image and your relationship with your body develops at an early age and sometimes, for instance, unkind playground comments can distort the picture you have of your body. If your inner resources of self-esteem and confidence are at a low ebb or underdeveloped, it often only needs one person to make one negative remark about your body and you tend to remember it forever.

Whatever your current shape, both physical and health-wise, your body is actually a miracle with its amazing collection of thousands of finely tuned parts and processes, all functioning more or less perfectly. Whatever your size, shape or level of fitness or health you can still feel good about your body when you develop an *appreciation* of its wonder and beauty – yes, it *is* wonderful – and, yes, it is *beautiful*, the beauty of perfect form and function, where everything works in harmony and balance.

When you appreciate your body in this way on a daily basis, you will find you automatically begin to regard it in a different light, taking more care of it, nurturing it and giving it what it wants and needs. When you appreciate your body you will find you automatically begin to make healthy and supportive choices for yourself. You will be drawn to nourishing your body with wholesome, fresh foods and, by honouring your body, you will be less likely to abuse or overindulge it in any way. Because you treasure your body you will also feel more inclined to exercise your body so you remain fit and supple all your days. You will also find you value regular hours and make sure you have sufficient rest at night; a peaceful, confident mind drifts off easily into deep and tranquil sleep. Best of all, after a night of peaceful sleep you will awake feeling good and bouncing with abundant energy.

There are millions of different kinds of attractiveness in the world, there will always be people who are currently regarded as the ultimate in beauty but the attributes of what is perceived by some as beauty change quite dramatically from generation to generation and from culture to culture; it is ephemeral – of no consequence. None of us can or need to compete. If we do, we set ourselves in a personally damaging, low self esteem, no-win situation.

So, the most important factor in having a good body image is to realise that you, the real you, is a beautiful and perfect person. Respect and cherish yourself, and treat yourself as though you are loved, then feeling good about your body will follow along naturally.

When you meet people you don't usually remember them just for the shape of their nose or the size of their hands. You recall what sort of person they are and how you relate to them. We all know when we have met a person who we like and trust, who exudes confidence and fun and we remember and value those aspects far and away above the colour of their eyes.

When you treat yourself with love and appreciation, confidence, calmness and an attitude of compassion to others will shine out from you, giving you a glow that reflects the beautiful person you are inside. Others will remember you, value and respect you for the genuine and real person you are. As you gaze straight at them, with confidence, inner peace and loving kindness, this inner beauty shining out of your eyes will be what is remembered.

Your self-worth is never dependent on any of your physical attributes. We are all different and are meant to be different. There is, therefore, no competition. Trying to be something other than yourself is to deny your own value and your own spirit. You are here to be you and you alone. Love yourself as you are. In doing so, you will come alive to yourself and to others and really feel good about being you.

11. Keep Moving!

There are plenty of steps you can take along the way to facilitate the process of feeling good about your body and to improve your body image. These range from changing the way you *think* about your body to the simple act of 'standing tall' which will instantly make you feel more confident and lithe. For the former, positive Bodymind Directions are what is needed, and for the latter try the Alexander Technique, Pilates or yoga which are invaluable for improving your posture and bringing awareness to the way you use your body.

Include in your approach some kind of physical activity, something that fits in with your current fitness level and your lifestyle. The many benefits of exercise are widely promoted, however exercise need not necessarily mean having to set an hour or two aside for an exhausting session down at the gym. Even a brisk walk will make you feel instantly good about yourself as exercise produces those wonderful endorphins, nature's own feel-good factor. The benefits of just ten minutes exercise can be measured in your body hours later, so walk to the school, the station, the shops or just take the time to enjoy a turn around the block.

The type of exercise you choose does make a differences; different exercise regimes have different aims and different effects upon you. For example, competitive sports can produce heightened emotions and good cardiovascular exercise, whereas exercise such as yoga can produce a calm, contemplative state and a relaxed body. Choose which type of exercise you feel you need, bearing in mind that a good balance of activities is important.

Most of us spend far too long in inactivity all day, some of us sitting for hours at a time. So try to make it a rule to get up and walk around or at least to stand up and really stretch every half hour or so to shake out those fixed joints. The safest way to exercise bodies unused to activity is in the water – and you don't even have to be able to swim. Join an aquafitness class or hydrotherapy class or just exercise, jump and run in the water. Twenty minutes of fun in the water will release endorphins, loosen your joints and make your heart beat faster which is great for your cardiovascular system and is essential for real fitness. If you can't get along to a pool try yoga, tai chi or Pilates, all of which use safe and gentle stretching activities suitable for all, especially the less able or those unused to exercise. These activities are also of benefit because they bring you into a calm state, similar to that in meditation.

The best way to exercise is to take part in an activity that you enjoy and preferably one that involves other people too. Professor Michael Argyle in his book, 'The Psychology of Happiness' suggests that exercise such as Scottish dancing or line dancing is the perfect way to happiness as it combines social activities, exercise, mental activity and enjoyment – all feel-good factors.

So run, dance, sing, make love – enjoy your body and what it can do. Keep moving and remain lithe and supple for the rest of your life. Keep moving and you cannot fail but to feel good about yourself.

Try The Shake Dance in the next section to energise you. It's fun, a stress reliever and good for your posture and joints.

12. The Shake Dance

For boosting energy, giving your whole body a work-out, relieving stress and strain and for pure fun try 'The Shake'. 'The Shake' is quite a demanding exercise and so build up gradually from a minute or so at first to perhaps ten minutes in all, especially if you have any physical problems. Unless your fellow workers are like-minded, it's probably best to do this exercise when you are alone!

Use 'The Shake' when you have been doing a repetitive activity where you tend to end up with hunched, tense shoulders, such as driving, working on a computer or on the telephone. 'The Shake' also has the power to relax the nervous system and the potential to break up patterns of anxiety and worry. So try 'The Shake' not only to invigorate yourself but to release muscular and mental tension also.

Take your shoes off and stand or sit in an upright chair. Take a few moments to get in touch with your body and send messages down to your feet to ground them. Let your breathing slow down and deepen.

Now, close your eyes and very gently start to move, rocking back and forth. Let your body find its own natural rhythm. Now begin to shake: start with your hands, then gradually bring in every part of your body, remaining aware of your feet being firmly rooted in the ground, and keeping your joints and muscles relaxed and loose. Concentrate on letting your movements become bigger and bigger, wilder and wilder. Let go and be totally abandoned. Pull faces, stick your tongue out, roll your eyes, make sounds, grunt, growl, squeak, shout, giggle, sing, be totally uninhibited. Move

around if you want to. Don't try to do any of these things – just let go and do whatever you feel like doing. Build up to a climax of wild movements, letting go totally.

You will know when you feel enough is enough. When you come to that point, suddenly STOP – feel the energy vibrations humming through you and let your body go slack. 'Come down' by centering your attention in your abdomen and by sending 'grounding' messages to your feet. Don't move until you feel perfectly calm and grounded.

The idea behind 'The Shake' is that at the final stage, you enter a similar state to meditation and your body rhythm pulsates at the same frequency as the earth's life force, thus charging you with natural vitality.

Whatever happens, 'The Shake' gives your body and mind a good work-out and there is no doubt you are charged with energy – and it's *fun*.

3

13. The Energy Dial

Energy needs vary throughout the day; for some activities you need instant high energy and for others you need very little energy. Sometimes you will have sufficient high energy for a particular task but sometimes you may feel your energy levels could do with a boost in order to perform the task. Conversely, sometimes you need to quieten and relax, such as when going to sleep and there may be occasions when this is no problem, but others when you feel wide awake and restless. These types of scenario are where the Energy Dial comes into its own. It's a simple and fun way to take hold of your own energy and increase or reduce your level as you need. Here's how to do it:

In your imagination create your very own special Energy Dial.

Your Energy Dial could be like a traditional clock with a normal clock face, with perhaps either a shiny modernistic chrome case or an old wooden case. Alternatively, the time could be marked by an arrow or a liquid travelling upwards, from 0–10, rather like a thermometer or a 'test your strength' machine that you hit with a hammer. Create your Energy Dial in whatever size, shape or form you like. Whatever your Energy Dial looks like, it will have numbers on it, 0 – 10, to represent your level of energy. When you have maximum energy levels the indicator or hand would be at 10, when you are asleep, the indicator or hand would be at 0.

When you want lots of energy and to feel full of vigour and life, imagine your Energy Dial going as high as you want it to, perhaps 8, 9 or even 10, depending upon how much energy you need at the time. Follow this by instructing yourself to increase your energy with an appropriate Bodymind Direction such as,

'Feel full of energy!'

When you want to relax and quieten down, visualise your Energy Dial going slowly back down to 2, 3 or 4, depending upon the level of relaxation you require. Give your Bodymind Direction,

'Slow down now, slow down................'

When you want to go to sleep at night, in your imagination turn the hands slowly back down through the numbers, 5, 4, 3, 2, 1 and by the time you get to 0 you will be asleep. Give your Bodymind Direction,

'Quiet now, perfectly quiet and relaxed. Go to sleep......................'

Repeat the Bodymind Direction as many times as is necessary to feel the effect you require. Remember to pause after each Bodymind Direction to allow the instruction to be passed on to your Bodymind Network and for you to feel the result.

Make the most of your Energy Dial and use it often, the more you practice with it the more effective it will become.

14. Breathing

The state of your breathing gives a good indication of the state of your emotions and your current mindset. When you are agitated your breathing will be quick and gasping, when you are calm or resting your breathing will be slow and deep. By becoming aware of your breathing you have a good guide as to how you are reacting to a particular situation. This is not the only useful aspect of being aware of your breath.

Breathing is one body function you can take hold of and change. Therefore, *you can change the way you think and feel by changing your breathing mode.* What excellent news! Your body assumes the physiological state of any particular form of breathing, so, when you breathe in short bursts at the top of your chest, your body and mind react by initiating the 'stress response' with all its characteristics, including the production of adrenalin. When you change your breathing to a slower and deeper mode, your body and mind respond by becoming more peaceful and calm and the 'happiness response' is initiated with the production of endorphins.

Most of us pay little attention to our breathing and we are inclined to take it completely for granted. Unfortunately, most people tend to breathe inefficiently and so miss out on the advantages of correct breathing, such as the production of endorphins. How are **you** breathing?

> **Check your breathing by putting one hand on your chest and another between the bottom of your rib cage and your abdomen. Let your hands rest there for a few minutes and then notice which hand moves the most.**

If your lower hand is moving the most you are breathing correctly. This is known as diaphragmatic breathing. Diaphragmatic breathing is the most efficient way to breathe for general use. If, instead of using diaphragmatic breathing you use the top of the chest muscles, breathing becomes faster, shallower and the intake of oxygen becomes more inefficient. Used habitually for normal activities, this type of breathing can even make you feel tense, headachy and unwell.

The deeper, diaphragmatic kind of breathing has many beneficial effects, such as:

Muscle relaxation.
Efficient cell cleansing to rid the body of impurities.
Effective use of the oxygen you breathe in.
Efficient regeneration of all the cells of your body.
Optimum function of many other systems of your body.
The production of endorphins – nature's feel-good factor.
Feelings of health and well being.

So, take advantage of all these benefits and retrain your breathing habits and nourish your whole being at a basic level by practising diaphragmatic breathing as described in the next section.

15. Breathing Practice

Use this method for practising your diaphragmatic breathing. You can practice lying down, sitting or standing. It is as well to practice in all three positions so that you learn how it feels to breathe diaphragmatically at all times.

1. Lie down on the floor or on your bed with your knees bent OR sit on a firm, upright chair, sitting with an upright posture to allow room for your rib cage and diaphragm to expand OR stand. Make sure your clothing is loose, especially around your rib cage, waist and abdomen.

2. Breathing through your nose, just observe your breath as it flows in and out. Notice the movement of your rib cage and abdomen. Don't do anything, just observe your breathing pattern. If you are lying down you may notice your ribs moving at the sides and your back expanding against the floor or bed. Sitting, standing or lying you may notice your ribcage expanding and falling at the side and the back.

3. Make sure your upper chest and shoulders are not moving, the only part of your body to move is the area around your abdomen, waist and lower ribs. Your diaphragm is a large muscle between the floor of your rib cage and the organs in your abdomen. When you breathe in, your rib cage expands at both the front and the back of your chest and the diaphragm moves downwards; when you breathe out, the diaphragm moves upwards and the stale air is pushed out of your body.

4. Continue just observing your breathing, for at least five minutes. Don't force your breathing mechanism in any way, just allow your breath to flow in and out quietly and naturally. Notice how you gradually become more and more relaxed and filled with feelings of well being as the endorphins flow. At the same time your body processes begin to function optimally and the healing processes are stimulated and enhanced.

3

Practice during the day, standing, sitting or lying down and soon this type of breathing will become automatic for you. Many people like to use this type of breathing practice as their main form of relaxation as it is so beneficial and pleasurable. The practice is similar to meditation but the aim and focus are slightly different as you will appreciate when you have tried both approaches. With this breathing practice you are learning about the way you breathe and deliberately paying attention to your body's movements in order to retrain your breathing. With meditation your breathing serves as a focus for your errant mind and the main aim is to notice whatever happens, accept and let go without becoming hooked into your thoughts.

Deep breathing is a gateway into relaxation and even more exciting, visualising easily and vividly which can lead into making real changes in your life. Read next how to develop this wonderful skill.

16. Visualisation

In the first section of this book (1:15) you were shown what an amazing ability you have for visualisation, or imaginative 'day-dreaming'. Check this out again to remind yourself of just how powerful your ability is to visualise.

Imagine a blue sky with your name written on it in gold letters.

Imagine hearing the sound of a drum.

Imagine the taste as you bite into a sharp lemon.

Imagine touching the soft furry coat of a cat.

Imagine the smell of a newly mown lawn.

Imagine the salty air of the sea and the surf rushing in to crash on the sandy shore.

Take a moment with each scenario and note what happens.

You probably 'saw', 'heard', 'felt' or experienced some other sensation with each of the scenes. The image or sensation was probably gone in a flash and you may be able to visualise one of your senses more vividly than others, but it doesn't matter. Visualisation of events, objects or places has great implications in your life. When you visualise, your mind does not know whether the image is real or imaginary. This means it makes no difference to the way your Bodymind Network reacts to the images. So, even if you are tired or feel a cold coming on, instead of telling yourself you are bound to be ill or lacking in energy, see yourself as being full of health, energy and vitality, tell yourself, *'You are full of energy and perfectly healthy'* and you will be far more likely to move towards that outcome.

The visualisations you experienced above were very brief and completed in your 'normal' mode of being. When you relax, your powers of visualisation grow and flourish even more. You enter a different realm where you have unlimited powers to influence and enhance your health and happiness. Visualisation can be used successfully even though you may think you don't have those kind of imaginative powers. It is a skill that has been lying dormant within you since childhood. With practice this ability can be restored to create the changes you want to generate a happy, fulfilling lifestyle and to transform the way your body functions. You can use the exciting technique of visualisation in a vivid and effective way to promote perfect health and happiness.

Try the following visualisation now to capitalize upon your inner powers to promote glowing health, vibrant energy and high self-esteem – your ideal you.

17. Visualisation – 'Your Ideal You'

There are various ways you can go through the visualisation. You may read it through a few times and then take yourself through it from memory, or record it yourself, or ask someone to read it slowly to you. The visualisation can also be obtained from the author at the address at the very end of the book.

Find a quiet place where you can sit or lie down for 20 minutes or so. Make sure you are warm enough and won't be disturbed. Take off your shoes and loosen any tight clothing, make yourself really comfortable.

Let your body sink down into the surface beneath you and allow your eyes to shut. You feel comfortable and warm, with nothing to do........... Breathe out and relax, allowing your breath to become slow and gentle.......... Feel your body becoming more and more relaxed, heavier and heavier. Allow your thoughts to float through your mind, just watch them go by. Enjoy the relaxing effect you are bringing about..........

Now, imagine being in a perfectly warm and safe garden, the sun gently shining down, birds singing in the distance. You smell the perfume from the flowers and grass. The garden is exactly as you would like it to be with green, newly-mown grass, flowerbeds of every shade and hue and beautiful mature trees.

You take a narrow winding path that leads to a particularly secluded corner of the garden where you come to a delightful clear, shallow pool. The surface of the pool is shining and smooth, reflecting the sky and the surrounding trees. The atmosphere is so tranquil and inviting that you sit down on a grassy bank in the dappled shade of a tree and think how wonderful it is to be here in this peaceful place.............

As you look at the pool you notice a shimmering golden glow on its surface......... a beautiful golden light slowly arises from the pool spreading its sparkling golden radiance around the whole

3

area. Now you notice that gradually the shining golden light parts in the centre............ it is as though a stage has been revealed.............

On this 'stage' you can see a person, surrounded by shining golden light like an aura, who radiates energy, health and confidence. This person is, in fact, **you**, as you would most like to be, full of all the qualities you would ideally like to have, looking your very fittest and at your most attractive .... but even more so. Your ideal self.

Continue to watch as you see your 'ideal self' doing all the things you would truly like to be able to do in your life. Creative and enjoyable activities that would make you happy and fulfilled, no matter how unattainable they may currently seem. You see your 'ideal self' acting with total confidence and enjoyment, full of energy and health. You bring loving kindness, compassion, optimism and fun to all your relationships and those around you respond with an open, co-operative and friendly manner. You handle all your daily proceedings, even those that may be more challenging than most, expertly and with good heart. Observe yourself moving around more thoughtfully, with grace, poise and calm confidence. Notice that you are speaking more slowly than usual with a low, calm voice. Your health is flourishing as you eat and act wisely, taking loving care of your body. All you do at work and play reflects your new inner spirit of happiness and confidence which shines out like a beacon........ you are joyous, vibrant and free.

This joyful, healthy, magnificent being that is your ideal is your POTENTIAL. You would not be able to see yourself in this way if you did not already have all these qualities and this potential within you.

And now the whole golden glowing radiance around the pool grows and grows until you become enveloped in the golden light. Your 'ideal you' moves closer and closer to you, the radiance surrounding both of you, until you merge together and become as one, enfolded within the beautiful light....................

Now you **are** your ideal self and you emanate all the qualities you have admired. You **feel** what it is like to be full of health............ you **feel** high in confidence........... you **feel** full of joy and vitality........... you **feel** excited and filled with pleasure at feeling this way. Yes, you feel **totally** good about yourself...................

Enjoy these feelings............ and whilst they are at their peak make a sign to yourself, if you haven't already done so in a previous visualisation this could be pressing your first finger and thumb firmly together, or choose some other signal. This is your secret sign, to anchor all those wonderful feelings within you. Later you will be able to recall these feelings whenever you wish just by making your signal again. Test the signal about ten minutes after you have finished the visualisation.

And now your relaxation grows deeper and deeper. You are totally bathed in peace and calm, surrounded by the golden light. The luminous golden glow cradles you and waves of peace are flowing around you..................... you are calm and still...................... filled with golden serenity and pure tranquillity...................

(leave a long pause here to enjoy the peace)

And then slowly, very slowly and, in your own time, become aware of the sounds around you and of your own room..................... Lie quietly for a few moments more..........be at peace, content in the knowledge that you have made a difference to your body and mind, you have nourished, stimulated and inspired yourself at a deep level..............

You can return to this magical pool at any time you wish, this peaceful place will always be there for you.

Very slowly stretch out now, stretch your fingers and toes... and then gradually start movement again, feeling full of all those wonderful qualities you have visualised, let the feelings carry on in whatever you do next feeling full of vitality, yet rested and peaceful............... keeping these feelings with you as you begin gently to go about your day........

When you go through the visualisation next time, make your signal as soon as you begin to feel really confident, excited and happy. Keep making the signal till the feeling almost peaks and then stop. By making your signal when the feelings are still increasing you ensure you fix the strongest feelings within you.

During the day, when you want to recall the powerful, confident and relaxed feelings you have enjoyed in this session, stop what you are doing for a moment, breathe out and relax and make your secret signal to yourself and enjoy the feelings of freedom and confidence and high self-esteem that are automatically released. Do this as often as you like, as the more you practice, the more effective the signal will become and the stronger the feelings of feeling good about yourself will be.

18. The Power of Bodymind Directions for Feeling Good About Yourself

The last section of 'Feel Good About Yourself' covers the power of Bodymind Directions for feeling good about yourself and for vibrant good health. As you already know, Bodymind Directions are an extraordinary power tool for transformation. These Bodymind Directions are aimed at supporting, valuing and appreciating yourself; especially on those occasions when you find yourself thinking negatively. **Turn that voice inside you into a friend who is on your side and not one who is against you.**

Remember, you are giving the Bodymind Directions *to* yourself, instructing yourself to move towards a particular course of action, which is why it's best to construct your sentences to comply with this. For example, instead of saying, 'My health improves every day', you instruct or direct yourself by saying, 'Your health improves every day'. Try it out and see the distinction.

Remember that after giving a Bodymind Direction you can intensify any response by saying, 'more and more', 'faster than this', or '..... is improving every day', or similar phrases of your own as appropriate.

NB PAUSE AND WAIT to notice any response after each Bodymind Direction.

Use the Tuning-In session first to still your body and mind. See Section 1 if you need to remind yourself of the process. Select just **three or four** Bodymind Directions that resonate with you right now, use them for a week or two and then notice the difference they have made.

Understand and accept that when you give Bodymind Directions you create the conditions in your body and mind for them to actually come true.

3

Bodymind Directions for Feeling Good About Yourself

'Breathe in and SMILE.'

'Feel powerful and strong.'

'Feel full of vibrant health and energy.'

'You sparkle with confidence.'

"Move with grace and suppleness, walk tall.'

'Breathe in health and happiness.'

'Listen to your body's needs.'

'Appreciate and love your beautiful body.'

'Enjoy life, have fun.'

'Love and accept yourself as you are.'

'Feel good about yourself – *always*.'

'You are safe and secure. All is well in your world.'

Bodymind Directions for Health, Pain and General Ailments

When you get a sore throat or any other ache, pain or condition, your initial thought is probably something along the lines of 'Oh no, I'm going to be ill/out of action', 'I've got a headache' or 'My throat's sore'. React immediately with positive Bodymind Directions. Don't wait, begin giving Bodymind Directions and continue with them all day. When you feel slightly 'off-colour' don't let that feeling establish itself – every time you think of your health, counter the thought with more positive Bodymind Directions. Be on your guard as negative Bodymind Directions percolate very subtly and efficiently into your psyche and take hold, giving undesirable messages to your body to which your Bodymind Network will respond by sending out signals that you are indeed becoming ill. To stop these messages in their tracks, counter this type of thought immediately with positive Bodymind Directions. Pay attention to your thoughts and be aware if you begin to give yourself negative Bodymind Directions again. Never forget that you become what you think, so, think happy and healthy thoughts in order to lead a happy and healthy life. It cannot be repeated too often that you are what you *think* you are. So think healthy thoughts – always.

As before, select or make up your own Bodymind Directions that are appropriate to your condition. Remember that Bodymind Directions should always be as short and succinct as possible and always expressed in the positive. Some examples:

> 'You *deserve* to be healthy.'
> 'Feel healthier and healthier every day.'
> 'You're getting better and better every day.'
> 'Your health improves every day.'
> 'Increase your energy more and more.'
> 'Let go of anything unwanted in your body.'
> 'There is no need for this condition to flourish.'
> 'Completely remove the negative conditions that are causing this problem.'

> *To use at night:* 'When you wake you will be completely rested and full of health.'

Remember, you unerringly move and grow towards that upon which you focus your mind. And so, focus always on discovering and nurturing happiness, health and peace of mind in every area of your life, using suitable Bodymind Directions to support you. By holding in your mind the ideal picture of how you would *like* to be performing in any situation in your life, you will make it easy for that image to come true for you – in other words, see yourself as being a happy, healthy person and you will *be* happy and healthy.

19. Review

1. **You** are the Thinker in your Mind and you can always choose which way you view your life, with either a positive or negative slant (3).

2. You are whatever you **think** you are. What you believe about yourself transforms your reality.

3. **Refuse** to dwell upon negative thoughts or negative Bodymind Directions.

4. Determine to replace limiting negative Bodymind Directions with uplifting, supporting Bodymind Directions. This is one of the most important decisions you can make (8).

5. Let your innate sense of goodness be the governing force in your life (9).

6. Remember that happiness is in the here and now, not at some future date when you have achieved/obtained something.

7. **You** choose where to place your attention and upon what you focus; and so choose interesting, absorbing pursuits, think happy thoughts and you will be outward-looking, inspire confidence in yourself and stay fulfilled and happy – the essence of feeling good about yourself.

8. Learn to appreciate your body. Treat it with respect in every aspect of your life from the way you clothe it, exercise it and nourish it (10).

9. Increase your energy levels (11–13).

10. 'Breathing Lessons' (14–15).

11. For sparkling good health, boundless energy, vitality and high self-confidence use the 'Your Ideal You' visualisation. Make it your very own powerful and inspiring therapeutic experience (16–17).

12. Choose a short selection of Bodymind Directions to nurture high self-esteem and boundless good health.

3

Follow your dreams

1. Your Purpose in Life

To achieve happiness and fulfil your true potential in life, you need to have a clear vision of your desires, something to aim for – in other words, a target or goal. Not the goal of 'being happy' or 'fulfilled' but goals purely to give shape and purpose to your life.

Having a purpose is a real requirement for a happy life, the tendency otherwise is to drift aimlessly, pushed and pulled by the forces around, feeling dissatisfied and unfulfilled, your mind filled with things you 'ought' to do rather than those you want to do.

If you can't think of anything in your life you enjoy doing, do something about it right *now*, as living like this can become a habit. Don't get used to the feeling of being unfulfilled. It doesn't especially matter what your goals are, whether making a special cake, breeding canaries, losing weight or crossing the Atlantic single-handed, the only requirement being that they are goals you truly and deeply desire.

You will find that once you have a goal to aim for it will transform the way you feel and think. With a goal, you immediately feel more in control of your life and your personal power is maximised. Your brain is an amazing biochemical powerhouse and when you focus on what you want, your mind sends a positive signal to every nerve cell in your body. When you attain your goal your confidence and self-esteem are multiplied.

However, you will realize it is not the achievement of the goal alone that brings deep happiness; happiness comes from each step on the journey you take towards the achievement of your goal. This is because happiness is always in the here and now, in the present moment, right on the very path you are currently taking. So, even as you are working on your goal you will feel that inner sense of satisfaction and pleasure that is happiness.

The achievement of your goal will lead you onwards, giving you encouragement to expand your horizons yet further, setting other or more ambitious goals. One of the secrets of a full and happy life is firstly to determine what you want and secondly, with this as a goal, to *act* upon it to make the goal your reality. This process is easily undertaken if you follow the format in the next pages. Read on to discover what it is you truly desire.

4

2. Seeking Your First Goal

In order to be realised, any goal needs to be very clearly detailed and set out because your Bodymind Network only responds to very simple and clear statements. The way to define your goals is through asking questions of yourself. In fact, the quality of your whole life is largely defined by the type of questions you ask yourself because the type of questions you ask will determine the answers you receive. If, typically, you ask negative questions of yourself, such as, *'Why does everything I touch go wrong?', 'Why can't I get it together to do this?'* or *'Why am I always off-colour and tired?'* you are almost bound to get limiting and negative answers. The answers would tend to be along the lines of, *'Because I'm hopeless'*. However, if you ask higher quality questions, such as, *'What do I need to do to regain my health?'* or *'What do I need to do to gain more happiness in my life?'* the answers will be constructive and build your self-esteem instead of negating you.

Eventually you may have goals in place for every area of your life, from your career, your health, your relationships to your leisure activities, personal and spiritual development but to start with it is best if you concentrate on one particular goal, something you *really* want; a main goal.

To discover this first goal you are going to contact your Inner Wisdom, that part of you deep inside which always speaks the truth and knows what is in your best interests. Your Inner Wisdom will allow you to clarify your desires and choose that which makes you at peace and brings you happiness.

In the general hurry and flurry of daily life it is easy to neglect your Inner Wisdom but, despite your preoccupation with your busy life, your Inner Wisdom is still there deep within you, just waiting for you to quieten and listen to its enlightened voice. In answer to your questions, this voice may reply to you in actual words or pictures in your head, sounds or subtle sensations of some kind from your body, flashes of intuition, or even just a simple 'knowing'. When you ask questions of yourself, always, always take note of the smallest and seemingly most insignificant changes within yourself, as this will be your body, mind or spirit giving their answer. Nurture your ability to listen to yourself in this way, as contact with your Inner Wisdom is your greatest source of power and strength.

3. Use Your Inner Wisdom to Find Your Goals

This technique will help you to clarify your deepest desires and discover your first goal.

Make sure you can be left in peace for about 15 minutes or so. Make yourself comfortable with plenty of paper and a pencil to hand.

Allow yourself to relax by being attentive to your breath, letting it become just a little deeper and just a little slower. Then, on each out-breath, allow your face to relax, and smile gently. This smile will relax you even more and send 'happy messages' to your mind and body. Now, be still and 'drop down inside yourself' and thinking of your life and everything you would like to be, do, or have, ask yourself,

'What do I want?'

Just relax, bring an open mind to the question and answers will come to you quite spontaneously. Write down **everything** that comes to your mind, no matter how far out of your reach any one thing may seem at the moment. Aim high, the sky's the limit and don't allow negative thoughts in. Set any limiting thoughts aside and write down everything and anything that comes to you.

Include anything you always wanted to do, and anything you've ever enjoyed and would like to start again, if you had the time or space. Let your imagination and Inner Wisdom run free, whether it's sailboarding, starting a new course, making new friendships, growing a herb garden, decorating a room, losing weight, getting fitter, or spending more quality time with your children. Whatever comes to you, write it down. The aim is to discover your dreams. No-one else will see the list, so let go, open up and admit your long held desires, whether they are 'every-day' or more enterprising projects. This exercise is for you alone and so there is no one else to please but yourself. Push through your 'comfort zone' and let your horizons be wide. At this time, don't concern yourself with **how** you will achieve any particular goal, just concentrate on writing down your desires. The 'how' comes later.

When no more answers come, ask the question,

'What else do I want?'

Keep asking this question. One answer may lead you on to another and so refer back occasionally through your responses. Free-associate between each area of your life:

Personal relationships.
Success in your work or career.
Your health.
Your pleasure and leisure time.
Joyous giving to others and the environment.
Enriching your spiritual life/personal development.

4

If you wish to expand your list, 'brainstorm' through your life, writing down all your strengths and interests, anything you loved to do as a child perhaps, or activities in which you know you are comfortable, confident and successful. Jot down everything, no matter how apparently insignificant. It may eventually lead to uncovering the thought of a career change, starting your own business or widening your personal interests. All these ideas and suggestions may lead you on to goals you had not thought of before.

Always construct your goals in the positive and make sure they have happiness and fulfilment at their heart and are used only for the greater good of all concerned. To work with the universal laws, construct your goals with happiness in mind and you will draw happiness towards you. You will then also be fulfilling your real purpose which is to live a life full of joy, peace, goodwill and well being.

Continue until you feel your list is complete and no more answers arise in your consciousness. You will eventually have a very long list of everything you **really** want to do, have, be.

Now that you have your list of potential goals, it's time to winnow them down to just one major goal.

4. Choosing Your No.1 Goal

1. Go through your list and ask of each potential goal,

'Do I **really** want this?'

If the answer is 'No', cross it through.

2. Go through your list again and ask this time,

'Do I want this goal very, very much, or do I want it just somewhat?'

Mark the items you want very much with a star.

3. Now rewrite your goals in two lists, List A, with all the 'starred' items and List B, with the remaining goals. Set List B aside for the moment.

4. Working on your 'starred' list, List A, if it has more than six items, look carefully through them and note the ones you **most desire** and then delete the ones you want less and write them on the other list, List B.

You will now have six items or less on your 'starred' list. From this list you can select your **ONE** most important goal. Look at the list and ask your Inner Wisdom,

'Which goal do I want the most of all?'

The answer you receive is your main goal.

The goal may fit into just one area of your life or it may overlap into two or more zones.

Into which main area of your life does your main goal fit?

Later on you can choose a goal for each of the areas of your life. Some straightforward or simple goals may be achieved side-by-side, but it is often best to concentrate upon one goal at a time or your focus of attention will be spread too widely and your energies become dissipated.

If you so desire, you can refine the goals that remain even further. Look at the items left on your 'starred' list and ask yourself which of those remaining goals you want most of all. This will give you your second goal. Do the same for each item left on the list until you are down to the last one. You will now have a plan for your next few goals in order of preference. Remember, though, priorities change and lists such as these should always be revised and refined before going ahead again.

4

For now, set all your goals safely aside for when you feel ready to embark upon another project. Now is the time to concentrate on your main goal.

Whenever you want to discover your true desires for any area of your life, use the same method to release your intuitive ideas.

5. The Success Route

The way to achieve your goal is by working towards it in a succession of small steps. The secret of success when planning to achieve any goal is to know exactly where to start and to have a broad idea of the main steps you will take. Each step is a mini-goal and you can celebrate your success with each mini-goal accomplished and so have continual feedback of achievement.

This next exercise will show you how to discover both your starting point and the main actions to take along the way.

In the centre of a separate sheet of paper draw a circle. In a moment you are going to write your main goal in the circle. When you write your goal it is vital you describe it as clearly and accurately as possible. It needs to be a statement of **exactly** what you want to achieve, in as much detail as possible, as this is your mission statement.

Ask yourself the following questions when refining your goal:

Exactly what are you doing?

Where are you?

What time of day is it?

Is anyone with you?

How do you feel?

How do you feel about it emotionally?

Is this goal in the interest of and for the highest good of all concerned?

How will you know when you have achieved your goal?

Write your mission statement inside the circle:

4

Sue and I are on a quiet road and we are running a mile three times a week after work. I am running easily and fluidly, I feel strong and proud of myself

Don't use negative statements, such as 'I am no longer unfit'. Your subconscious mind tends to ignore small words such as 'no' and homes in on bigger ideas, such as 'unfit'. So, keep your goal totally positive, simple and clear.

Next you are going to use your inner powers to get inside the sensation of already having achieved your goal. This will help you to discover the steps that lead up to achieving your goal.

6. Using Your Inner Powers for Goal Success

Now for the exciting moment when you achieve your goal – this time it is in your imagination only, but remember that what you can conceive in your mind, you can achieve in reality. Doing this exercise will show you the steps you need to take to make that goal come to life.

1. Have your piece of paper with your mission statement for your goal alongside you and also have a pencil and some spare paper to hand. Take a few quiet moments to relax your body and mind by concentrating on your breath and allowing it to slow down. Feel yourself becoming calmer and more 'centred' within yourself as you do this.

2. Now, read your mission statement a few times, repeating it slowly and with real feeling, as though the words were really true for you right now this minute. Let the words fix themselves into your mind, see them on the page very clearly as you repeat them.

3. Feel yourself becoming even more calm and 'centred', be very still and then imagine yourself as you will be when your goal is already achieved. Make the images or sensations really bright and clear, it's a perfect day and you feel strong and confident. See yourself and your surroundings as vividly as you can, your clothes, the sounds, scents, colours and textures around you. If you are painting, see the paint and paper, the colours and your wonderfully creative picture. If it's weight you want to lose, see yourself in the mirror in beautiful new flattering clothes, look down and run your hands over your body, feel your new slenderness under your hands, hear the compliments you receive. If you are running, smell the fresh air, feel your legs pounding the ground, feel your breath coming evenly and strongly and see the views around you. Whatever your goal, sense and see it fully. Really live it. See yourself with a happy smile and know you can easily achieve this goal and any other you truly desire. Be proud of your success and know you have the confidence to achieve success

and fulfilment in any area of your life.

4. Now take just a few more moments to look back and analyse just how you would have achieved your goal. Go back through the steps you would have taken to arrive at that place of success. Ask yourself, what was the very first step you would have taken? And the next? And the next? Continue like this, in your imagination, until you reach your goal again. In this way you will discover the stages you need to take in order to reach success with your goal.

5. Repeat this Bodymind Direction to yourself inside your head or aloud,

> 'Your goal or something even better is now materialising. You are ....' (painting with creativity and enjoyment/running four times a week – repeat whatever is your goal).

And then, for even more emphasis, say,

> 'YES!, You are ....' (repeat your goal).

You could also add this supportive and affirmative Bodymind Direction:

> 'It is EASY to ....' (your goal).

6. Finally, take time to congratulate yourself and to feel genuine pleasure at achieving your goal, feel a glowing sense of being successful and happy.

7. Gently return your attention to the surroundings around you and feel alert, relaxed and filled with warm contentment at knowing now that you really can achieve your goal.

8. While fresh in your mind, jot down on your spare piece of paper the steps you took to achieve your goal.

Note Bodymind Direction No.5, 'Your goal or **something even better** is now materialising............'. It's necessary to say 'or something even better' as, although we *think* we know what it is we truly want, we may not be aware of many of the possible effects and consequences of working with this goal. So, because Bodymind Directions are powerful, it is as well to put in this extra clause and so leave it to your Inner Wisdom to decide exactly what is in your best interest.

Create enough space in your day to include the few moments necessary for using this exercise to bring your goal to reality. When you imagine and sense your success in your mind or your body, your goal is certain to become into being.

Really get inside your dream and know every move you will need to take. Keep with you that positive sense of certainty about achieving your goal that you felt during the exercise. You **can** do it and you **will** do it.

7. Preparing to Achieve Your Dream

For this exercise you will need a pencil and piece of paper with your mission statement written in the centre of a circle in the middle of the paper.

Make sure you can be undisturbed for a short while and take a few moments to withdraw from your surroundings and concentrate on your breathing. Allow each out-breath to become slightly longer until you are breathing quietly and slowly. On each out-breath, allow yourself to smile gently. This will help you to relax and centre yourself. Now you are going to contact your Inner Power to discover the practical steps you will need to take to achieve your dream. You already have the outline from the previous step. Ask yourself what you actually need to do to achieve your goal. When a response comes to your mind, jot it down around the circle. Ask yourself questions such as 'When? Where? How?' for each item that comes to you. Some of the items can be connected with a line as one step leads into another, for example, referring to the previous illustration of painting the following may come to mind:

Get painting materials.

What sort? Write the answer. (Paints, brushes, paper.)

What kind of paint, brushes, paper? Write the answer.

Where from? Write the answer.

When? Set a date and mark it on your calendar.

What to do next?

Eventually you will come to the final 'What to do next?' question and the answer will be –

TO BEGIN

Goethe said,

'Whatever you can do or *dream you can*, begin it.
Boldness has genius, magic and power in it.
Begin it now.'

8. Pushing the Walls of the 'Comfort Zone Bubble'

Going through the process of searching for and working towards goals requires a great input of energy, as does any change. You may find the whole process a real challenge. This is because you are currently living within your 'comfort zone', and moving outside of that zone can be distinctly *un*comfortable for a while. Changing something means taking risks to some degree or other. Not doing anything, but accepting the status quo, means you stay within your 'comfort zone'. This is the area of life within which you feel safe and 'at home'. You could regard the comfort zone rather like a bubble surrounding you. Inside the bubble everything is known. Life inside the bubble is filled with all the activities you normally do, some almost without thinking about them, such as walking, driving, having old friends round for a meal and so on. To achieve these activities you once had to push against the walls of your bubble – you were, maybe, slightly apprehensive at first but you continued pushing until the activity felt comfortable – you stopped falling over when you tried to walk, driving became effortless, your new friends became old, well-known friends with whom you could feel relaxed.

To move out of your comfort zone bubble you face risks and challenges – you think you might make mistakes, be let down, be emotionally upset, get tired, lose money or feel 'not good enough' in some way. Inside the comforting enclosed world of 'staying the same' you avoid those fears. Although living inside the bubble you are cushioned from some fear and mishaps, you are also totally limiting and restricting yourself and it actually *stops* you from achieving the things you want – and you will find that fear and mishaps have a nasty habit of sneaking in anyway. People who choose to stay within their comfort zone bubble make excuses for why they haven't achieved what they say they want, 'I haven't the time/energy' or 'I can't do that because........'. Their comfort zone in these circumstances tends to contract, the bubble becomes smaller and smaller and as less is attempted they become more and more dissatisfied and breed fresh fears. The comfort zone has the capacity to contract so much that you barely dare step outside; it also has the potential to expand infinitely.

4

By pushing against the walls of your comfort bubble and bringing new and challenging elements into your life your comfort zone expands. When you push against the walls of your bubble often enough any new activity soon becomes easy, the apprehension evaporates and your bubble grows. The confidence generated by your success also increases and spreads to support you in other new areas of endeavour. The more you push, the bigger your comfort zone becomes, your world increases and you become more outgoing and confident as you push through any fears and doubts. Of course everyone needs the basic security of a comfort zone but to do things you really want to do and to release yourself from situations you don't want you need to push the walls of the bubble to reach that bigger, exciting and fulfilling world which is even more comfortable and enjoyable.

The one thing you can be sure of is that your fears evaporate as you face them. Next time you feel the tingle of fear, apprehension or doubt, feel it, ignore it and then do what you want to do anyway – and watch how the tingle disappears and see how your bubble of familiarity, comfort, confidence and security expands. So, push the bubble often and hard, and watch as you feel more and more fulfilled.

9. Taking the First Step

Now you know your goal, you have your mission statement and an outline plan, you have your paints, brushes and paper (or whatever you may need for your particular goal)................ but, you have yet to make a mark on the paper (or whatever is your first step to your goal).

Courage! Now is the moment to sweep away any mental blocks you may feel are hindering you. This is the time doubts creep in and your comfort zone bubble seems too cosy and friendly a place to leave. Release yourself from the hold of those negative thoughts and move on through the fear. You with your inner powers are stronger than those thoughts (see Section 3 to remind you about your automatic negative Bodymind Directions and how to counter them). Any kind of change is challenging – even desirable change. So, push the walls of your bubble, break through the resistance and turn those fearful feelings into feelings of excitement. Change from, 'I'm afraid I'll fail' into, 'This is so exciting!'

So, take courage, be bold, you know what you want to do.....
You know how to go about doing it....
Now you are ready actually to begin.

This is an exciting and wonderful time for you.
This is your moment.
Begin NOW!

10. 'Total Fulfilment' Visualisation

Your goal will be brought nearer to you every day when you use this imaginative visualisation because, as you remember, you move unerringly towards whatever it is you constantly think about, visualise or sense in your body. So, the repetition of strong images and sensations of success make your goal's reality ever more sure.

Trust your instincts and your Inner Wisdom, anything that comes to your mind in the visualisation is valid and relevant, so always go with the very first images that come to you.

As before, there is a choice as to how you use the visualisation. It is best either recorded on to a tape or read aloud to you by a friend. If these are not options, read the visualisation carefully and then 'take yourself through it' using the main ideas. A prerecorded tape is also available from the address at the end of the book. Where you see a dotted line, leave a pause for the effect to be felt.

Make sure you will be undisturbed for 15–20 minutes or so. Make yourself very comfortable in a quiet, warm place, with your head rested. Take your shoes off and loosen any tight clothing. Rest your hands on your abdomen, not touching, or at your side. Have your goal at the back of your mind.

**Close your eyes and just allow yourself to 'be'. There's nothing to do, nothing to think about, just be. Be with your breath as it rises and falls. Notice how, with each breath, you are becoming more and more relaxed. Be with your body as it becomes heavier and heavier and sink down into the surface below you...............
You are becoming more and more comfortable, and more and more at ease.................**

Become aware of your breathing and for a moment or two just notice the regular and gentle rise and fall of your abdomen as you breathe in and out..............

You can allow your breathing to become a little deeper and a little slower.......

(Long pause.....)

Your breath is the key to deep and powerful relaxation..........

**As your breathing slows and deepens your body becomes more and more relaxed, peaceful and at ease.............. Feel the soothing waves of relaxation begin to move through your body. ....
...........just let go..............**

(Very long pause)

And now give yourself the Bodymind Direction 'Relax and let go', say it to yourself once or twice, either out aloud or inside your head.......................... and feel yourself **totally** relax and let go.........................

Notice how still you have become and how quiet your body is apart from the gentle rise and fall of your abdomen. You have brought warmth, comfort and peaceful relaxation to all of your body.............

(Long pause)

And now, with each breath you let go of any thoughts.................... they are of no concern to you here and now..............let them pass by without affecting you in any way.......................... just let them go.................................... Now you are free, free from tension and free from your thoughts, you feel totally peaceful and calm............

As you go on your inner journey, there's nothing to do, just relax and let my words float around you. Don't worry if your images are different from the ones I suggest, use whatever pictures come into your mind, your own pictures and images are always right for you.

And so, you find yourself on a path in a beautiful garden............. the day is fine and just the right temperature for you. Feel the gentle breeze on your arms................. the perfume of flowers is in the air............ Feel the peace in this garden...... it is a very special place.......

Look down at your feet now and see the surface of the path. You may see pebbles, gravel, bricks, moss, grass or some other surface.................... And now you look up at the trees and see how their branches link gracefully overhead from one side of the path to the other. The soft sunlight throws dappled shadows on to the ground through the leafy trees......... There are beautiful flowers blooming either side of the path. You stop for a moment and watch them as they move gently in the breeze. The delightful perfume of the flowers floats across to you........... roses.......

honeysuckle .... lavender .... You stand quite still and listen................. and now you hear the sounds of the garden .... in the background you can hear the watery sounds of a stream as it splashes and gurgles on its way.............perhaps the rustle of tiny animals in the undergrowth, the song of many different types of birds............................ You reach out and touch something, it could be a flower, a tree, an animal. You feel totally relaxed in the friendly, warm atmosphere here, you feel free and at peace.................

As you walk you leave all the noise and bustle of day-to-day events and situations behind you............................ the further down the path you walk the further away you are from every day life, you leave it all far, far behind and go deeper and deeper down into peace and relaxation...........................

Now the garden opens out ahead of you and you come to an expanse of beautifully mown, brilliant green grass. In the centre of the lawn you see a Golden Globe, which is just a little taller than you, sparkling in the sunlight. You walk towards the golden sphere and see a curved door in its side. The Golden Globe is for you only, and as you approach, the curved golden door slides open to welcome you. You step forwards and pass into the Golden Globe through a shimmering, sparkling waterfall of light. This dancing radiant cascade of white light dances all around you like an aura, it uplifts and protects you and you know that everything that takes place here is in your best interest and for your highest good.

The Golden Globe is much larger on the inside than it seemed from the outside. The light is gently diffused and everything inside is a soft golden colour. In the centre of the Golden Globe is a carpet woven from golden threads. On the carpet is a magnificent and splendid golden chair gleaming in the light. The golden chair is made to suit you exactly. Sit in the chair and lean against its supportive back. The chair is wonderfully comfortable. You close your eyes..........and relax................... and let go completely.......... (long pause).

You sense that every part of your body is being refreshed, restored and invigorated in this special seat...........Every cell of your body is relaxed, content and working smoothly and easily...............You are nourishing and energising yourself.......ready for success in whatever you do.

On the curved wall opposite the chair you see a huge screen, this can be operated from the remote controls you now find in the arm of the chair. This is the Golden Globe Dream Machine where you can rehearse and plan the future, to make certain that your dreams come true. With the Golden Globe Dream Machine you can LIVE the future now.

In the arm of the chair are buttons for travelling backwards or forwards in your life, to see the past, present or the future. There is also a special larger, golden button which you will use later on. Today you will use the button for going to the future. For now, think of your current goal, the one you already have in your mind.............. get ready to see yourself going through the stages leading to that goal............... You are going to see yourself a short distance along the path to your goal, it may be some time later to-day or it may be perhaps two weeks time. It's up to you. Then you will see yourself a little further along the path and then finally completing your goal.

So now press the remote control forward button to go a short distance into the future. See yourself on the screen at that time in the future and find out what you will be doing towards achieving your goal. Make the picture as big and bright as possible, fill in as much detail as you can. Which particular step are you taking towards achieving your goal? What exactly are you doing? Is there anyone with you? What are they doing or saying?

Now relax again and let that picture fade away. Now press the forward control button once more, and this time go further into the future and find out which stage you are at now. Again, what are you doing? Who else is there? What is happening? Make the picture as detailed as you can.

And now, let that picture fade away and relax again.

Now, press the forward button once more to the time when you actually achieve your goal. See yourself as you will be at that time. The day is perfect and everything is just right for you. You feel strong and confident, full of satisfaction and pride knowing you have achieved your chosen goal by your own efforts. Whatever your goal is, watch yourself as you carry it out with ease and confidence. Notice what you are wearing, see the colours, hear the sounds. Take in as much as you can about the whole scene.

And now find and press the special gold button on the remote control. This gold button will allow you to **be** yourself as you will be when you achieve your goal. You have seen the future – now press the big gold button and **LIVE** the future, live it, as though you are taking part in your goal activity right now, not just on a screen in front of you............. **feel** it in your body. If you're running............ you feel yourself running.................... if you're leading a meeting, feel yourself being in charge and full of energy .... if you're gardening, feel the earth in your hands................ painting, see the paints and feel the brush between your fingers................ whatever you're doing feel it in your body.................... The day is perfect and everything is just right for you. Have a real sense of what is going on around you. Look down and see what you are wearing, hear the sounds, smell the aromas and feel the textures around you. Visualise and sense as much as you can about the whole scene.

Feel yourself smiling and feeling exhilarated, enthusiastic and excited. Feel proud of yourself for accomplishing your goal and know you can go on with confidence to achieve even greater success and fulfilment in any area you choose. This is not the end, it is another beginning.

And now, to crown your achievement, you hear applause – people are applauding your success, it could be anyone you have ever known, family, friends, acquaintances, people in shops, on trains, in buses, in aeroplanes, on motorways everyone everywhere seems to be clapping and applauding your success...............
Enjoy the acknowledgement and praise of your achievement for a moment.................. Experience the fullness of your achievement................

You feel confident, relaxed and happy...............feel yourself filled and expanded with the inner abundance of realising your dream................ As you brim over with these wonderful sensations, make a secret signal to yourself, perhaps by pressing your thumb and a finger together (if you have not used this signal previously) to anchor those sensations, then, later on, you can re-live the feelings merely by making your signal again.

Now that you have seen and lived the future, repeat a positive Bodymind Direction to yourself.

Say to yourself,

    'You are now fulfilling your potential.
    You .... (fill in your goal) with ease and success.'

(Pause and wait for the Bodymind Directions to register with your Bodymind Network.)

And now, relax again................ and let any images fade away..................... and then return to having an awareness of your body. Now, slowly and gently, in your own time, open your eyes and look around you. In a moment stretch your fingers and toes................. gently stretch out your body, arms and legs .... and, when you are ready, begin movement again, taking with you all the wonderful feelings, ideas and images from this visualisation.......... Feel peaceful and calm, yet alert and ready to go about your day taking these feelings of relaxation and enthusiasm back with you. **Know** you can successfully achieve this and any other goal of your choice. Be filled with the image of successfully achieving your goal. Be sure to return to the garden with the Golden Globe many many times to reinforce and strengthen your resolve to reach your goal.

That is the end of the visualisation.

About ten minutes after you have finished the visualisation, 'fire' your anchor to check it and relive all those exhilarating feelings of success once again. Use your anchor often to recreate these feelings and to keep your intentions in focus.

Use the visualisation every day, step right into your dream and live every stage you will take to achieve your goal and to savour its accomplishment; it is certain then to become your reality. Keep these positive feelings of certainty within you to ensure you achieve your goal.

This empowering visualisation can be applied to any goal you like, in any area of your life, from leisure activities to career development, from health issues to relationships. When you use the visualisation, envision what you would like each particular part of your life to look like, what you would be doing, how others would respond to you, what would happen.

As you go about your day, act as if your desired goal is already with you. Imagine that you *are* your future self and bring the feeling into your life now. As you know, that about which you constantly think draws its reality nearer and nearer, as your life comes into line with your thoughts. By acting as if you already have something you create the inevitability of that abundance to be truly yours –

so...........

LIVE your dream.

11. Keeping on Track

You have started off on your new journey, full of excitement and filled with good intentions and so to keep the impetus high and your commitment firm consider using some or all of the ideas and reminders below:

1. Keep your desire for the goal high. Every day use the illuminating and inspiring 'Total Fulfilment' visualisation in the previous section.

2. Jump on negative thoughts by changing them into encouraging and positive Bodymind Directions. Change 'I don't think I can do this' to:

> **'Be easy on yourself.'**
> **'You are doing great and success is just around the corner.'**
> **'Keep going – you're nearly there.'**
> **'Determine to achieve and you *will*.'**
> **'You *deserve* to succeed.'**
> **'Relax and let go, there's no need to struggle.'**
> **'Your goal or something even better is materialising now.'**

3. Re-read your mission statement and then write it down on a piece of card. This can be your Incentive Card so keep it in a prominent place where it will be a constant reminder of your aims. Place the card where you will see it and read it often. You become used to objects being in one place and with familiarity they fail to register upon you so vividly. Change the position of the card occasionally so that it takes you by surprise and you read it anew.

4. Talk to others and seek guidance, inspiration or assistance. People are generally delighted to be asked for their opinion or suggestions as it shows you value and respect their knowledge. But, remember that you don't have to take their advice!

5. Every day, when you awaken and before you arise, ask yourself,

> *'What do I do today towards achieving my goal?'*

Then make sure you create or set aside the time to do that work.

6. **Ask yourself if you really truly want this goal.**

   If you don't, let it go immediately and move on to your next goal.

   If you do – take the next step, there is no other choice.

7. **If you're feeling lethargic or sluggish – do something!**

When you find yourself giving excuses like, 'I'm too tired/busy/lacking in energy to work on my goal' – the answer is to *move*! Do *something*. Don't wait for the energy to come or the 'right' moment. Anything at all will do, from taking a walk to tidying a shelf.

If you have 'writer's block', tidy your files, make notes, write one word, just one, and another will then follow. If you have 'artist's block', sharpen your pencils, clean your palette, do a sketch, read through your scrapbook or notebook – do anything to get yourself going again. If you feel too apathetic to get up for your run, sort out your gear, clean your shoes, check the map for a new route – again, do anything around the goal to make you shift that energy block.

When you make a move you benefit physically from the actual movement and psychologically from the achievement of the task. So *make* the move – the energy will be there for it – energy follows the demand. You ask for energy, and it is given, you make that first hesitant step and then another and then another until you are 'up and running' again. Try it next time you feel sluggish; ask for energy and surprise yourself with the result!

Try these Bodymind Directions to get you going:

   '**Come on .... (your name). You are *full* of energy. Your energy is increasing more and more with every move you take.**'

8. Whatever you do, don't let the goal become an obsession so that the process of achieving it is not enjoyable. It is the process,

the journey towards the goal that matters. Remember that happiness and fulfilment are in the process, not just in the achievement of your goal. So be gentle with yourself and with others and do it with love. *Enjoy* the journey.

12. Bodymind Directions for Achieving Your Goal

Use positive Bodymind Directions to keep your commitment high and determination to achieve your goal strong.

Remember that after giving a Bodymind Direction you can intensify any response by saying, 'more and more', 'faster than this' or '..... is improving every day' or similar phrases of your own.

Use the Tuning-In session first to still your body and mind. See Section 1 if you need to remind yourself of the process. Select just **three** or **four** Bodymind Directions that resonate with you right now, use them for a week or two and then notice the difference they have made.

Understand and accept that when you give Bodymind Directions you create the conditions in your body and mind for them to be realised.

The more you use your chosen Bodymind Directions the faster they will become your reality.

Choose three or four of the following Bodymind Directions or make up your own.

NB PAUSE AND WAIT to notice any response after each Bodymind Direction.

'Breathe in and SMILE.'
'You sparkle with confidence.'
'It is *easy* to .... (your goal).'
'You are worthy of success.'

'You *deserve* to succeed.'

'Enjoy life, have fun.'

'Determination is yours.'

'Keep going – you are nearly there.'

'You are filled with boundless energy.'

'Your goal or something even better is getting nearer and nearer every day.'

'This is so exciting!'

'Success is within your grasp.'

'You are open to receive limitless abundance and the reality of your dream.'

'Be proud of your successes and know you continue to achieve more and more each day.'

'Your goal is now materialising.'

'You .... (your goal) easily, with pleasure and enjoyment.'

'Relax and let go, there's no need to struggle, it's all happening beautifully.'

'It is easy to achieve this or something even better for the highest good of all concerned.'

13. Review

1. Create long and short term aims for each area of your life. Initially, work with one goal at a time, building up to making goals for each area of your life: your relationships; your job or career; your contribution to society; your leisure activities; your health; your spiritual development and your connection with nature; and your personal development, that is, creating inner peace and high self esteem.

2. Write down your desires and list what you would have to do to make them reality.

3. Ideally 'visit' each area of your life each day, but don't worry if you can't, remember that it's overall balance you're after.

4. The key to success is *action*. Take your life into your own hands. Determine what you want and *act* on it, don't wait for it to be given to you. Push through your 'comfort zone'.

5. Use the 'Total Fulfilment' visualisation often.

You already have the knowledge inside you of how to achieve success – you have had this from the very beginning of your life, from taking your first steps onwards. Now you can realise these inner powers and strengths and use them with awareness to achieve anything you want.

4

Fill your life with love

1. That Loving Feeling

Ideally, your path through life is meant to be such that you are a vital, joyful being, flowing from one choice to another with ease and grace and coexisting with your fellows in harmony and peaceful accord. A way of life where you dispense your time wisely, view events dispassionately and make your commitments skilfully so as to free up the more creative and dynamic life-enhancing powers within you. Your actions are kind and generous, both towards yourself and those who are in your life.

This ideal way of life begins and ends with just one very simple factor – loving. Being loving and compassionate towards others and benefiting from the return of those feelings occurs naturally to those who are firstly loving and compassionate towards themselves. If you cherish and nurture a loving, understanding attitude towards yourself the radiance you create spreads outwards to encompass all who come within your orbit. Having a loving attitude towards yourself is essential for giving out truly loving and compassionate vibrations to others and for enjoying those feelings in return.

A loving attitude towards yourself isn't the self-love that is full of over-weening pride, selfishness or self-importance. It is a love of understanding, forgiveness, approval and kindliness towards yourself. It is caring for your health and body with nutritious food, sufficient rest and adequate exercise and fresh air. It means not criticising yourself or others and accepting that you're fine just as you are but can make positive changes if you wish. It means not being resentful or blaming but being patient and kind to yourself when things don't go quite as you'd planned. It means taking the time to savour the pleasures of your successes, no matter how small. Self-love is not pride and vanity, which are defence mechanisms, self-love is enriching and cherishing. It means keeping your thoughts directed towards the positive, not either dwelling in the past or the future with 'if only.......' type of thoughts and wishes, but living in the present moment, truly aware, truly alive. Don't wait till you achieve 'that weight loss' or 'get that new job', or 'win that match', give yourself the love you deserve *NOW*.

5

2. More About Loving

Imagine for a moment what it would be like to love yourself totally and unconditionally.

If you truly loved yourself and your heart was filled with an attitude of loving kindness towards yourself, would you:

Be more supportive of yourself?
Laugh more?
Be less critical of yourself?
Be more understanding of yourself?
Be more tolerant of yourself?
Treat yourself with compassion?
Be less angry with yourself?
Have more fun?
Be less demanding of yourself?
Be less of a perfectionist or less careless?
Work harder/less hard?
Eat differently?
Take greater care of yourself?
Exercise more/less?
Listen to and honour your real needs?
Dwell less in the past?
Not be anxious about the future?
Change something about your work or relationships?
Think approving thoughts about yourself?
Really like yourself?
Praise and reassure yourself?
Feel good about yourself?

Loving includes all these things and more. Loving is not:

anger
jealousy
perfectionism
anxiety
selfishness

hatred

greed

resentment

criticism

bitterness

over-weening pride

vanity

defensiveness

guilt

or any other negative emotion or trait.

These emotions and traits are based on fear, the other side of the coin to love.

True loving is enriching and totally unconditional. It is not dependent upon how you behave, perform or what happens to you or whether or not you come up to any expectations you may have of yourself. True loving fosters confidence and enthusiasm. When mistakes are made you look at them and yourself with compassion and understanding. You treat yourself and others kindly, gently and with respect.

Read on to find out more about how to nurture love.

3. Decide to be Loving

Love itself is a feeling, but to be loving needs *action*. In every moment you can choose whether what you do is done lovingly or otherwise. If what you do is done lovingly it will be for the greater good and will produce a loving, life-enhancing and enriching feeling within you; you will feel good about yourself, glad to be you. If it is done 'otherwise' it will give you a displeasing feeling inside and make you feel unhappy and unloved. Which of these emotions you feel is your choice because the power is yours to determine how you will act in each and every moment. So, you can see that to be loving needs both *action* and also a *decision*. A decision as to whether to be loving or not.

If you decide you do want to be loving but are still not really sure how to do it or what it means, it really is very simple. To be loving is not a big 'earth-moving' thing to do and there aren't necessarily major decisions to be taken. The choices you make are often rather mundane, every day choices. Even ordinary decisions, such as what you choose to eat, can be done in a loving, caring way. Each and every small decision can be a choice between loving and being kind to yourself or otherwise.

The key to being a loving person is to decide to do something in a loving way whether or not you actually *feel* loving at that moment. The decision and action of doing something in a loving way will promote the loving feeling itself. So, beginning with yourself (as this is the first rule of loving), *decide* to be loving towards yourself, *act* in a loving way towards yourself and *do* loving things for yourself.

Think about how people behave when they are happy and when they love themselves and then you do the same. Act as if you accept yourself, act as if you are joyful, *make* yourself feel positive and optimistic with uplifting Bodymind Directions, smile, laugh, be kind, be gentle, be truly yourself at all times – and then the feeling will come. Let being happy and loving yourself become a habit. Deliberately decide to be loving and joyful and then act that way.

The same idea can be applied to any other way you want to feel. If you want to be positive and optimistic, ask yourself how you would behave if you were the kind of person who was positive and optimistic, then act that way and you will *be* positive and optimistic. If you want to be compassionate, act as if you were already a compassionate person, the same with enthusiasm, confidence or any other attribute. Act in the way you desire and then you will feel the appropriate feeling. So act lovingly and you will feel the feeling. The more loving and happiness you generate the more there will be, it's an upward spiral which increases limitlessly. The more love you feel, the more you *will* feel. So decide to start acting that loving feeling *right now.*

These are the kind of questions you need to ask of yourself if you wish to foster acting in a loving way. Ask any of the following types of questions often:

> 'How would I behave if I was being kind to myself?'
> 'How would I feel if I was a gentle, loving person?'
> 'What would I do here if I loved myself?'
> 'How would I behave if I was a generous person?'
> 'Which of these would I choose if I loved myself?'

'How would I go about this if I was confident?'

'How would I do this if I was a compassionate person?'

'How would I behave here if I respected myself?'

Create your own questions relevant to whatever situation you are in at the time, using any other appropriate words, such as unselfish, joyful, etc.

To reinforce your decision, feed yourself positive Bodymind Directions.

Remember to stop and pause after each Bodymind Direction in order to feel the feelings generated.

'Be kind.'

'Love yourself.'

'Accept yourself.'

'Approve of yourself totally and unconditionally.'

'Love yourself totally and unconditionally.'

'Accept yourself just as you are.'

'You are a fine and wonderful person.'

'You are deserving of love.'

'You're good enough just as you are.'

'You're filled with love.'

'You're full of understanding and compassion for yourself.'

'Cherish yourself.'

'Be joyful.'

'Be totally filled with happiness.'

Continue to nurture that loving feeling with the Loving Meditation in the next section.

4. A Loving Meditation

As you may have discovered in Section Two, the practice of meditation allows your mind to become calm and concentrated. This makes it a powerful tool for healing and for bringing joy, peace and love to your life. When you 'go within', as during relaxation exercises and meditation, you find that your very core, your very being *is* love. You don't really have to do any more than 'go within' to find that love. In finding it, you will then have the strong desire to want to share that love with others as well as the sensation of loving and being connected to all other beings and life forms. The more you practise with your meditation, the easier it becomes to regard yourself and others with love until, eventually, it becomes your normal way of being.

You cannot ever have too much love in your life, but love is not outside of you, love is within you. If you find you crave or desperately need loving from someone outside yourself 'to make you feel OK', realise that you are not in line with the first principle of love – *you first love yourself in order to love others and to receive love.* When you love yourself your whole attitude and approach to life changes. You laugh more, you have more fun, you are happier and more tolerant, you live with grace and feel complete. When you live your life in this manner you will be lovable, so others will be drawn irresistibly to you, loving you in return.

However, we don't always have an accepting and loving attitude towards ourselves. Too often we may be critical of ourselves, or feel inadequate or negative about ourselves in other ways, sometimes perhaps even feeling as though we are not 'good enough' to deserve love. In fact, for some people it may be quite a surprise, or even a shocking thought, to think they *could* love themselves and that it is more than OK to do so.

This 'Loving Meditation' highlights and consciously directs loving feelings to yourself so you can bring so much love, peace and tranquillity to your being that any hurts in your life can be healed, allowing you to recharge yourself and clear the way for a future of peace and happiness, free from the past.

In addition to these wonderful effects you will also find the meditation can be spiritually awakening. Within yourself you have energy that operates at four different levels. There is your basic physical energy, then your emotional mental field, at a more subtle level your mental energy field and at a finer level still, your spiritual energy level. Your spirit is the part of you which is connected with all life. All is one – and one is all, so, when you refresh either your body or other energies with relaxation or meditation, you also feed your spirit. The different levels are fundamentally the same energy and so meditation or relaxation applied to one level affects all. As this powerful and deep meditation enhances your physical, emotional and mental energy levels it consequently leaves you with a sense of being filled with love and peace and at one with life itself; a spiritual experience.

Try this meditation and see how wonderful it is to feel truly loved and deserving of love. Read the meditation through a few times to assimilate the ideas within it, or record it for yourself, leaving plenty of long pauses where appropriate.

Find a quiet place where you can be uninterrupted for a short while. Be comfortable, but in a position where you can remain alert. Ideally, sit on a straight-backed chair or cross-legged on the floor. Have your hands apart from each other either in your lap, or on your thighs.

Close your eyes and, for a few moments, just observe your breath as it flows in and out. Breathe naturally and normally and soon your body will begin to quieten. If you notice tension in any part of your body, breathe into the area and then allow it to relax and soften on the out-breath. Let all thoughts pass through your mind without reacting to them in any way, just let them float through your consciousness; this is the essence of meditation.

Continue to be mindful of your breathing for a few moments longer and then, when you begin to feel calm and peaceful, begin consciously to direct feelings of kindness and love towards yourself. To foster these feelings, bathe yourself in loving Bodymind Directions. Be gentle with yourself and choose those Bodymind Directions that most help you to pour love into your heart. Choose from the following suggestions for Bodymind Directions or use your own.

Remember to pause after each Bodymind Direction to allow time for the effect to be felt.

'Love yourself.'

'Accept yourself.'

'Be filled with love.'

'Feel only kindness towards yourself.'

'Respect yourself.'

'You are full of compassion.'

'Be free from anxiety.'

'You are kind and generous.'

'You are free from anger.'

'Be totally open and filled with understanding and compassion for yourself.'

'Love yourself, you are a wonderful being.'

'Be free from suffering.'

'You are confident and enthusiastic in all you do.'

'Love and approve of yourself.'

'You are a fine and wonderful person.'

'Cherish and love yourself.'

'Be joyful.'

'Love yourself totally in this moment.'

'You are filled with happiness.'

'You **deserve** love.'

'You are good enough just as you are.'

'You are filled and surrounded by the golden glow of love.'

'Relax your eyes........ relax your mouth..... and s..m..i..l..e.......'

Continue giving yourself loving messages until you feel as though you are overflowing with love. You will find this exercise a powerful and moving experience.

And now, continue with the meditation by sending these or similar feelings to someone you love, someone close to you. Visualise the person you hold dear as you send some loving Bodymind Directions to them. Compose your own Bodymind Directions to suit the person concerned. See the person surrounded with a shimmering golden aura of love and happiness.

'Let .... (name) be happy.'

'Let .... (name) feel joyful.'

'Let .... (name) be free of pain and suffering.'

Continue to give appropriate Bodymind Directions until you feel ready to move on.

Next, widen the sphere to include others you know and care for, perhaps your friends and family. Repeat similar Bodymind Directions appropriate to them and visualise them in the same way as before.

Now, focus on someone whom you do **not** hold in great affection, possibly even someone who has caused you pain, hurt or harm in some way.

Wrap yourself in compassion and love and send out healing to that person. To do this, let go of any resentment or dislike of the person and try to view them as someone who is also suffering, someone who also has feelings and who may be a victim of their background or upbringing. Can you understand why they behaved as they did? If someone has wronged you, they had their own reasons for it, see if you can see the situation from their point of view. This is the time to be generous and deliberately evoke feelings of compassion and kindness towards that person. See if you can find some good in the other person; if you look hard enough, you will find it. Let go of your own feelings and have only forgiveness in your heart. Look dispassionately, as an observer, at the events and energies of that time. Your anger, righteousness or resentment only hurt you, so it is no hardship to let these feelings go, you benefit from their release. You could regard a hurtful event as a learning experience from which you have taken what you need and which it is now time to let go.

Be of good grace and have only compassion and charity within you as you set the person free. See the person wrapped in healing love, like golden gossamer and see them becoming smaller and smaller. Then, finally, before you leave them there in the past, ask the person to forgive you for any hurt or harm caused to them by you, either knowingly or unknowingly. This at last will release you completely from this experience in your life, leaving you whole and able to move on. See the person recede now, as you move away from the past, see them become smaller and smaller until they are just a tiny golden dot, then watch as the dot itself is lost from view.

Thinking well of others is deeply beneficial to you, it is immensely liberating and makes you feel good in yourself. Feel yourself filled now with calmness and serenity and bring that feeling of wholeness and completeness away from the past and back to the present.

If you feel the need, take a moment to direct a few more Bodymind Directions towards yourself. Do so until you feel that the love in your heart has expanded so much you can now direct these feelings to anyone else who may be in need of kindness and caring.

Now move on to embrace all of life with love; the plants, the animals, Earth itself and even the entire Universe.

Your heart is now full, full of warmth, generosity and loving kindness towards yourself and all life. As you sit, bathed in love, you will feel a part of everything, a 'oneness', whole, complete and totally at peace.

And then, when you are ready, gently return to your own being, become aware of your breath and feel the contact of the surface beneath you. Do not be in a hurry to resume your day. This is a powerful meditation and a deeply spiritual experience during which, in your heart and mind, you can come to enjoy the great release of letting go of past feelings. You can do this whether the person is still alive or not. The meditation allows you to come to terms with your life and your place in Life itself. As the strong and positive feelings of understanding, compassion, acceptance, letting go and love generated towards yourself during this meditation are directed towards others, the way you view hurtful events is transformed. You heal not only your own hurts but also any painful events and difficult relationships in the past.

This meditation opens your heart to yourself and all beings and as it does so, the effects are profound. You come to see that everyone is deserving of more understanding, kindness and love, including yourself, and so your relationships will flourish. Any difficulties will be less likely to develop as you become more aware and more tolerant in your relationships, whether at home, work or socially. Practise this simple, yet powerful meditation often to enrich your whole life. The more you practise, the more loving and complete you will feel, in touch not only with yourself in a deep, compassionate and kindly way but with all around you.

5

5. How to Nurture that Loving Feeling

In this section you can hear about another way to nurture that loving feeling. Within you, and all others, there is a smaller, younger version of how you were as a baby, toddler or young child. As adults, we still carry around with us this more naive and immature version of ourselves which reacts to situations as we would have done as a child. The emotions and feelings you felt at that time are now exactly the same as they were then. The younger you, like any baby or young child, needs constant love and approval to thrive and grow. Your younger inner self, as with your present inner self, can never have enough loving and approval, it's impossible to give it too much. However, this younger self is often neglected and sometimes its presence is not even recognised at all. Did *you* know there was a 'little you' deep inside you, holding up its arms, crying out for love, affection and reassurance? This 'little you' is in desperate need of love and security and if it doesn't get it, it begins to panic and tries to get the attention it needs from others, possibly by manipulating them and playing 'power games' in order to get the love it craves. However, if you rely entirely for your well being on receiving love and approval from others, you are living with a false sense of security, because others can stop loving or remove their approval. Another way your inner child may demand your attention is by bombarding you with anxious or negative thoughts in order to get your reassurance and approval. You often only become aware of the child within when you become ill, upset or sleepless and cannot understand why. This little person is clamouring for your love and attention.

Once you realise you haven't been paying much attention to 'little you' it is easy to give your younger inner self the love and security it wants. It needn't seek attention in unwanted ways any longer, you, as a mature and loving adult, can take care of all its needs. When you give 'little you' the attention it wants, like a baby or young animal, it will be happy and quiet and no longer disturb you with undesired behaviour; all the unwelcome traits will melt away.

At first, when you give the younger version of you the attention it needs, you may need to be patient, until your 'little child' gains confidence in you and you can clearly hear its 'voice'. After all, it may have been neglected for a long time, so needs the space to recover its trust in you and to realise you *can* give it all it wants. As you begin to communicate with your younger self, you will find that, as with all children, there will be a certain simplicity, an innocence and freshness in the views of your child. Understand, it is a child looking at the world in an inexperienced and open way, without the baggage of adult emotions and preconceptions. Most people have set aside the more childlike aspects of themselves and have become serious, with a loss of that fresh way of looking at things. They tend to become staid, with set beliefs and attitudes, and sometimes even lose the capacity to find enjoyment and fun in situations. So, with the exercises that follow, you will not only be learning to love yourself, but will also be discovering how to tap into this rich source of creativity, sensitivity, clarity of view and fun to lighten up your life.

Your task in the exercises is simply to project loving feelings towards the little child within, to ask questions and to listen, listen and listen some more to what your child has to say. You can never pay enough attention to its wants. It will soon tell you when it is feeling secure in your love and approval.

When you have a strong commitment to love the child within and pay regular attention to that child, you also feel secure and confident. This child within *is* you. No-one can take away this inner joy and security, it is your own, created by you and, therefore, not dependent upon the vagaries and whims of others. And then, as your own love flows through you, true, unselfish, unconditional love, you become filled with so much love and confidence that it flows onwards to enfold others in its soft embrace. As your self-love and inner security increase and build, your capacity for loving: loving others, nature and life itself, grows proportionately.

Read on to discover how to get nearer to and love the inner version of the younger you.

6. Visualisation with Your Inner Child

Can you imagine seeing a tiny young child, standing in front of you, eyes big and wide, perhaps a little worried or frightened, chubby arms stretched up to you, wanting only one thing from you – to be picked up, held close, tears wiped away and to be loved?

It's an instinctive feeling to want to comfort and love that child. With the following visualisation you can now grow every bit nearer to your own inner little child and become like a loving parent to it, one who only ever has the child's happiness and best interests at heart.

Try this visualisation now. It is best either recorded or read to you by a friend. If neither of these suggestions is convenient, read the visualisation very carefully and then 'take yourself through it', keeping the main points in mind.

Make yourself comfortable in a place where you feel safe and can be undisturbed for a short while. Close your eyes, relax and let go. Let go of your thoughts, let go of your emotions and release all tensions from your body. Feel totally and completely relaxed.

Now, see yourself walking down a beautiful, long, country lane. It's a lovely day, the birds are singing, the sky is blue, the leaves on the trees are moving gently in the breeze, wild flowers are growing in profusion at the side of the lane. The further you walk, the further behind you leave the day. As you walk on you eventually come to a gate. You open the gate and see on the other side a flight of ten stone steps. At the bottom of the steps is a door set in an old stone wall. Go down the steps now and, as you descend, with each step you go deeper and deeper into relaxation. You are going down...... going down...... there are just five steps left now............ Five...... four............three............ two........... one............ You are now standing in front of the door set in the old stone wall.

You open the door and step through into the world of your younger self. You take in the whole scene. What are the surroundings? What is your younger self doing? What is your younger self feeling? Call to the child and watch as he or she runs to you, arms outstretched. See how happy the little child is to see you. Bend down and pick up the child, hold it close and speak to it gently and with great tenderness. (You may even feel like putting your arms around yourself at this point.) Tell your little child how much you love it, no matter what it may do. Soothe and comfort the child. Praise it and say how good it is. Let the child know that now you have made contact, you promise you will always be there for it and ready to listen to what it wants.

5

Love and hug this child and then, as the child begins to relax and accept you, say to it, 'Tell me anything that is bothering you'. Now listen to what the child has to say. Listen quietly and carefully. Take notice of any sensations, words or thoughts that come to you, this is the child's answer. Whatever the reply, love and reassure your child some more. Tell it you will always care for it. Have as long a conversation with your child as you wish. Continue with the dialogue until you are sure your child is content and reassured........................... (pause for as long as is needed).

When you are ready, kiss the child on the head, then gently put it down. Tell the child you love it and will be back to see it again very soon.

Now, let the warm waves of love that are flowing from you and which link you forever to this child soften your heart and bring gentleness and compassion to YOU. Feel this infinite love flowing around you, cradling and nurturing you like a warm, golden glow. Resolve now to stay in contact with your little child and to reassure it with loving kindness as often as you can. Remember that the little child **is** you, and this boundless love you feel is **yours** and is for you, just as you are, with whatever faults you perceive you have: this is true compassionate love.

Now, gradually and gently become aware of the surface beneath you and of the room around you and slowly bring movement to your body again. Return to the day overflowing with loving kindness towards yourself and surrounded with the glow of love from your warm and peaceful heart.

Use this visualisation often, at least once a day when you first make contact with your inner child. Cherish and nurture this new relationship, don't let your little child feel neglected again, as the benefits from this contact are infinite.

7. Healing Emotional Situations

In order to be able to be truly loving, feel whole and move on in life you may need to develop an attitude of forgiveness towards someone or something. An attitude of forgiveness releases many emotions, including resentment, guilt and anger. If these negative attitudes are harboured they block your ability to be loving and open. With their release comes empowerment and the ability to open your heart to all, including yourself.

You may find it challenging to consider forgiving some particular things, so do remember that for forgiveness, the attribute you need is the **desire** to forgive, you don't have to love, like or condone the person or act. Also remember that you are the one to benefit when you forgive as the act of forgiveness is a process of letting go, it sets you free and allows the past to stay where it belongs.

Try one or both of the next exercises to resolve a situation. This is especially appropriate if you find you are feeling irritated or upset with someone and seem unable to clear the issue.

'Throw it Away'

> Take a few minutes by yourself to write the whole event down in
> full detail. This will help to clear your mind. Write everything, all the
> factual incidents and all your emotions. When everything has been
> written down, don't read it through, tear the paper up and throw it
> away or burn it. As you do so, say calmly, 'Go in peace'. Feel the
> great sense of relief as the burden is lifted from you.

After the exercise use some Bodymind Directions to enrich the act of
forgiveness. Remember to pause after giving each Bodymind Direction
so that the effect can be noticed in your body, mind and spirit.

> 'Forgive and let go.'
>
> 'Release anything that is not love from your life.'
>
> 'Let harmony and peace fill your life.'
>
> 'You are free of the past.'
>
> 'All is well in your world.'

After this exercise, you may feel it is now possible to meet or to write to
the person concerned and effect a reconciliation.

Forgiveness will always give you a sense of freedom and
release because it is an act of love which opens your heart as you let
go the hurts from the past.

Seeing the Good

As it is not always possible to meet the person to heal the situation, or
if the matter is still unsettled, you could continue to work towards
resolving it with the following exercise. It is useful to realise that often
that which you dislike in others is an exact reflection of something you
may find difficult to accept in yourself. This is why forgiveness towards
others is so liberating for you. As you forgive and accept them, so you
promote an attitude of forgiveness and acceptance towards yourself.

In this exercise it might be helpful to work with pairs of
'forgiveness statements' or Forgiveness Bodymind Directions so that as
you forgive someone else you also forgive yourself for the same
'transgression'.

Remember to pause after each Bodymind Direction to give time for your Bodymind Network to be activated.

Forgiving the other person:

'Forgive .... (name) for ....'

Forgiving yourself:

'Forgive yourself for ....'

For example:

Forgiving the other person:

'Forgive Sally for being irritable and impatient.'

Forgiving yourself:

'Forgive yourself for being irritable and impatient.'

These Bodymind Directions work in two directions. With a forgiving attitude towards yourself you tend to become more understanding of others; and when you forgive others, you free up your own loving and life-enhancing feelings.

It would be a beautiful and loving thing to complete the whole process by spending a little extra time to seek out the good in the other person. You may have to almost force yourself to find good points about the other person, but when you look for the good in others you will find it. It only need be one point to begin with. Be wholehearted, warm and generous about it, it won't help you if it is done grudgingly with poor heart. The effort is 100% worth it. When you concentrate on finding the good in others you will discover it is reflected in the way they behave towards you. So, by changing how you feel towards someone, the way they act becomes a reflection of your own beliefs. You will also find that now you will attract people who behave towards you in a way that promotes a fulfilling, happy life. It is the same law that says 'give love out and love will return to you a thousandfold'. The type of relationship you have with the outer world reflects directly the type of relationship you have with yourself.

So, try the Bodymind Directions again, this time rounding off the process with an added Bodymind Direction affirming the good in the person or situation.

This is a particularly useful exercise for you to do last thing at night before you go to sleep. It clears the day and sets you up for a peaceful night's sleep and a fresh start to the next day.

For example:

Forgiving the other person:

> **'Forgive Sally for being irritable and impatient.'**

Forgiving yourself:

> **'Forgive yourself for being irritable and impatient.'**

Affirming their good:

> **'Sally is cheerful and fun to be with, she is loving and giving.'**

This last Bodymind Direction will transform your relationship with the other person and will also direct you towards the same good you now affirm in them. You change your attitude to the other person, and your attitude towards yourself is automatically changed along with it. You will discover that the negative aspects of yourself weaken and the good that is in you increases in abundance. Your world will become a delightful and pleasant place, the people you attract within your world will be loving and kindly, showing their best side to you. All of this because of a shift in *your* attitude.

In the next section you will find how to transform your close relationships with a very special way of giving a loving hug.

8. Hugging and Loving Meditation

Sometimes it's difficult for people to find the space in their hectic lives to give adequate nurturing time to the ones they love, often resulting in feelings of guilt. If you are rushed and hurried when you hug a friend, partner, or family member, the hug will have a distracted, perfunctory quality to it, reflecting your own state. The hug may even be just a gesture, with no depth or meaning to it. These underlying feelings are easily transmitted to and felt by the recipient of the hug, although they will say nothing.

Now you can transform your hugs into the most deep and loving hugs imaginable and the person receiving the hug will know the hug is given with real love, warmth and affection.

This simple and quick way to bring quality loving to your relationships is achieved by using breath awareness, a form of meditation. As you know already, the process of meditation brings you right into the present moment, the now. It is the key to achieving inner peace and to nourishing you in mind, body and spirit. When you are present, in the moment, your real self, your inner love shines out. You have an aura of peace, sincerity and tranquillity about you which is observable by others. You don't even have to practice this meditation; just do it and notice the difference it makes to the relationship with your loved ones.

5

Firstly, bring your attention to your breath and be fully aware of being in the present moment. Then, while you are hugging the person, breathe two or three times, being fully aware of each breath as it flows in and out of your body and of being in the 'now', fully conscious of both yourself and the other person. When you do this you become real and truly alive and the person being hugged will also feel real and alive to you. Even in this brief time your senses will be heightened and you will notice far more about yourself and the other person than ever before. The hug will be wonderfully meaningful and you will be totally aware and awake as to how precious is your loved one. This is **real** loving.

If the other person also knows about breathing and hugging, the hug will be doubly momentous as the two of you breathe together and become as one, in that minute.

So now, instead of giving a cursory hug when you see your family, friends or relatives, make the greeting a memorable moment, possibly even one of the best moments in your life, being totally aware and alive to them in that moment. This is the essence of loving.

9. Loving, Giving and Receiving

Your real purpose in life, your true adult status, is to *give*. When you were very young your purpose was to receive, to receive all you needed to become a rounded mature human being; sufficient love, shelter, food, warmth, clothes, education, fun and many other essentials. The attribute of giving to others develops as you progress through life, as you learn to share what you have. Giving *is* loving and true giving, as with loving, is without expectation. Giving with the heart is a joyful experience where you don't expect anything in return, not even gratitude. It is unconditional.

The more you give, the richer and happier your life will be, because when you give love, or when you are generous, or when you spread happiness, you don't 'give it away' and leave yourself with less, you retain a 'copy' for yourself. So, the more you give, the more you receive, both from others and from the feelings flowing inside yourself. Giving and receiving are like two sides of the same coin.

Loving, giving and receiving are part of a cycle. Keep the cycle going by loving and giving more and more and more. Giving is always in the present moment, so give as often as you can. Every moment, every moment of 'now-ness' is an opportunity to contribute in some form. You don't have to bestow all your possessions, although a few do so in an extreme gesture of giving and simplicity. But we, no doubt need to continue to work, earn our living and contribute to our family life. So, you need to think of how you can give of your time and energy for others. What you do doesn't matter, provided you are doing *something* for others – often.

Gratitude and Appreciation

Expressing gratitude is another form of opening yourself up to love, whether it is gratitude voiced directly to others, or, asserted inwardly. For instance, in the form of a simple 'thank you', you might say directly to the person concerned,

'Thank you so much, I'm so grateful to you for doing that.'

Or you could make a conscious choice to express your thanks inwardly, to yourself,

'I'm so grateful to .... (person) for doing that.'

Always proclaim your gratitude fully, wholeheartedly and with real feeling and meaning. The more sensitive you become to all the good in your life, the more joy you will experience in your life. Positive thoughts and actions will draw more positive thoughts and actions to them, joy will attract more joy, a smile will attract more smiles and so your abundance will grow.

Expressing your thanks is always, as with loving and giving, experienced in the *present moment.* It would be appropriate to regard each 'present' moment as, indeed, a present, a gift, as it is always an opportunity to give and receive, whether it is love, joy, happiness or something more material. So give yourself 'the present' when you do this next exercise which is a wonderful way to foster the habit of expressing your appreciation and gratitude. When you acknowledge that you value the simple things in life you come straight into the 'present' moment and open up your centre of joy and happiness. It is an excellent stress-reliever in times of adversity. Although any time of the day would be a good time, it is particularly appropriate to either begin or end the day with gratitude and thanks.

5

Give yourself Bodymind Directions, either out aloud or inside your head, and, as always, make sure you pause after each one so that the effect is fully registered in your body and mind. You should feel an opening, an expansion inside yourself which increases with each statement of appreciation.

'Be thankful for .... '

Complete the sentence with as many blessings from your life as you can and feel yourself overflow with warmth and love as you become thankful and appreciative for life itself.

Here are some ideas of how the sentence could be completed, but do invent your own:

'Be thankful for your loving friends.'
'Be thankful for having sufficient to eat.'
'Be thankful for the air you breathe.'
'Be thankful for the plants and animals.'
'Be thankful for the ability to feel joy.'
'Be thankful for life itself.'

Don't be deceived by the seeming simplicity of this exercise. It is a powerful and transforming procedure and one to be repeated often, at least once a day, to nourish your very being.

10. Bodymind Directions for Loving

Use powerful and positive Bodymind Directions to open your heart centre and to bring love to your life.

Use the Tuning-In session first to still your body and mind. See Section 1 if you need to remind yourself of the process. Select just **three or four** Bodymind Directions that resonate with you right now, use them for a week or two and then notice the difference they have made.

Understand and accept that when you give Bodymind Directions you create the conditions in your body and mind for them to become reality.

Remember, you are giving the Bodymind Directions **to** yourself, instructing yourself to move towards a particular emotion or course of action. This is why you need to construct your sentences in the third person, like an order or command. This makes it easily accepted by your Bodymind Network.

The more you use your chosen Bodymind Directions the faster they will become your reality.

Remember that after giving a Bodymind Direction you can intensify any response by saying, 'more and more', 'faster than this', or '..... is improving every day', or similar phrases of your own.

Choose three or four of the following Bodymind Directions or make up your own.

NB PAUSE AND WAIT to notice any response after each Bodymind Direction.

'Breathe in and SMILE.'

'Appreciate and love yourself.'

'Love, respect and cherish yourself.'

'Focus always on loving you.'

'You love yourself totally in this moment.'

'Make joy and happiness be at the centre of your world.'

'Joy is always within you. Connect to it NOW.'

'Build your life around happiness and joy.'

'Be filled with joy and express happiness.'

'Accept and appreciate the good in your life.'

'Be thankful for all the simple joys in your life.'

'Love yourself.'

'Be loving and giving.'

'Receive with graciousness and gratitude.'

'Respect yourself – you *deserve* to be loved.'

'Forgive and let go all that is not love in your life.'

'Let the past and future go – be here now, in the present moment where joy resides.'

'Accept the present moment as a gift and an opportunity to love and to give.'

'Enjoy life, have fun.'

'Love and accept yourself as you are.'

'Feel good about yourself – *always*.'

'You are safe and secure. All is well in your world.'

'Let harmony and peace fill your life.'

'Be filled with loving kindness now and always.'

'Love yourself totally in this moment.'

Use the Bodymind Directions often during the day as the more you focus on what you *do* want in life, the nearer you grow towards that ideal. So, focus totally on loving yourself and the good in your life. Nurture that loving feeling so that love flows out from you in all directions, giving its healing warmth to all on your path. Remember that your true purpose in life is to *give*.

11. Review

1. An ideal life begins and ends with being compassionate and loving towards yourself and others.

2. This loving feeling can be nurtured, you can make a *decision* to be loving.

3. In order to love others, you first need to love yourself. Foster this love with the 'Loving Meditation' and by developing a loving, understanding relationship with your younger inner self.

4. Develop an attitude of forgiveness to open the way to joy and loving. Use either or both of the 'Forgiveness Exercises' to release past hurts and to find the good in others.

5. 'Hug and Love' for a *real* loving experience.

6. Develop an attitude of gratitude and appreciation, both of others and of the simple things in life around you.

7. Remember that in life the true adult status is to *give*.

8. Use appropriate Bodymind Directions to develop gratitude and to build giving and loving as the centre of your life.

Summary

Feel-good Factors

The whole of this book is centred around the 'Bodymind Connection', the amazing conjunction between mind and body, where each one influences how the other functions. Every thought you think resonates at cellular level, creating either a positive or negative effect, and in reverse effect your body posture can influence the way you feel, again with either a positive or negative effect. You can use this knowledge to bring about any changes you may desire, by means of the 'Bodymind Directions'. The ability to use this knowledge is the key to true happiness.

Read the 'Factors for Feeling Good' below and hold them in your mind, because what you choose to think about really does decide your reality. This is not merely an idealistic fantasy; with the enlightenment and support of the ideas in this book, feeling good and happiness can be true for you. The ideas and techniques will show you how to find the peace and happiness in your life *now,* fulfilling your happiness potential, allowing you to walk the golden path of happiness through your life. So, although this book is at an end, life, loving and finding peace and happiness are ongoing processes. From now on, this book is not a book to read, but a book for you to **USE**. Enjoy using it.

Factors for Feeling Good

These are some of the factors for feeling good, they are not given in any particular order.

Read them often – act on them always.

1. **Choose** to be happy, happiness is a **decision**.

2. Be governed always by your natural inner sense of goodness, your higher self, your Inner Wisdom.

3. Recognise that **you** are in control of your life, your thoughts and your feelings. **You** are the Thinker in your Mind, and you are whatever you **think** you are. Use the phenomenal powers of your Inner Wisdom in conjunction with Bodymind Directions to promote happiness, inner calm, enhanced spirituality, better health and brilliant success in all you do.

4. Do that which makes you feel at peace with yourself.

5. Be open to a rich variety of experience.

6. Develop new skills and keep on learning every day of your life.

7. Develop strong commitments to *all* the different areas of your life, from your health, relationships, job, leisure activities, inner spiritual development to contributing to society and the wider world.

8. Have clear aims for each area of your life. The key to success is *action*. Determine what you want and *act* on it.

9. Find enjoyment in all tasks, even those that are tedious and difficult.

10. Learn to concentrate and sustain your attention on the task in hand – then you will enjoy every experience.

11. Regard setbacks as a challenge to be overcome.

12. Be outward looking. Focus your attention upon the outside world and those within it rather than upon yourself and your own emotions.

13. Live in harmony with your environment and know that you are a part of everything around you.

14. Be compassionate and loving towards yourself.

15. Forgive and let go of past hurts, nurture an attitude of understanding and compassion towards others.

16. Develop an attitude of gratitude and appreciation of others and the simple blessings of life.

17. Remember always that true adult status is to *give*.

18. Inner peace and happiness are always to be found right here, right *now*, never at some time in the future when you achieve or obtain something you desire.

19. Be here *NOW*.

An order form for the tape which accompanies this book is on page 184.

Index

acceptance 161
adrenalin 109
affirmations 14
aggression 73
aims *see* goals
Alexander Technique 104–5
anchor signal 41, 115, 116, 142
anger 85, 152, 159, 165–8
anxiety 60, 87, 88, 152, 162
   and Shake Dance 106
appreciation 172, 174, 178
approval 85, 102, 151, 161, 162
Argyle, Michael 105–6
assistance 143
attention 178
   to inner child 162
   in listening 70–1
   in meditation 67–8
attitude 91–2

beauty 103–4
bitterness 152–3
blame 71–3, 74, 78, 151
body 11, 103–20
   care of 151
   image 103–5
body language 48–50, 177
'Body Smiling' 55–6, 80
Bodymind Connection 2, 9
Bodymind Directions 14–16, 43, 58
   automatic 87–9, 92–4
   cancelling of 18
   control of responses 17–18
   and energy 108, 144
   and feeling good 86, 116–20
   and forgiveness 166–8
   and goal achievement 141, 145–6
   and health 117–19
   and inner peace 78–80
   and Inner Wisdom 42
   instructions for 22, 23
   and love 154, 155, 157–61, 172–4
   and mantra meditation 68–70
   negative 87–9, 92–100, 117–19
      see also thoughts, negative
   positive 96–7, 104–5, 119, 143
   see also question and answer
      system; Start-up Bodymind
      Directions
Bodymind Network 11, 43, 67
   evidence for 13–14
   and goals 123
   instructions for 12, 14–16, 101
   interaction with 12
   and mantra meditation 68–70

power of 14
   and questioning 26–7
   see also Bodymind Connection
brain 11, 50, 123
   left side 31, 60
   right side 31, 61
'Breathe and Smile' Mantra 50, 80
   and Bodymind Directions 51
   and daily activities 53–5
   and walking 53
breathing 109–11
   and 'body smiling' 55–6
   diaphragmatic 109–11
   and endorphins 51
   and goal achievement 132–3
   and meditation 60, 63, 157, 160,
      169
      focus of 65–8
   and mindset 109
   and relaxation 32–6, 51, 110–11
   and visualisation 38, 136
Buddhism 59–60, 72

calm 43, 47
   and Bodymind Direction 17, 23, 177
   and Higher Level Communication
      System 31
cardiovascular system 105
career 142, 146, 178
cells 88, 110, 123, 177
challenges 134
change 133–4
'Comfort Zone Bubble' 133–4, 147
commitments 143, 178
compassion 153, 154, 178
   and ideal life 151, 174
   and inner child 165
   in listening 71
   and 'Loving Meditation' 159, 161
   and meditation 62, 64, 66, 68
   and relationships 73, 74
   and thought patterns 94
   and understanding 72
concentration 178
confidence 85, 99, 103, 104
   and Bodymind Directions 17
   and goal attainment 123, 134
   and love 153
   and visualisation 112, 116
consciousness 64–5
contentment 22, 57
control 75
creative visualisation techniques 2
creativity 7, 47, 162
criticism 94, 152–3

dancing 105–6
defensiveness 152–3
diet 24, 29, 119, 151
dreams and desires 2, 121–47
    achievement of 132–3, 146

emotions 24, 32
    and body language 48–50
    negative 152–3
endorphins 31, 36, 50, 105
    and breathing 109, 110, 111
    and positive vibrations 88–9
energy 85, 102, 156
    block 144
    and body image 103
    and Bodymind Directions 16
    creative 7
    and goal achievement 133, 144
    and inner peace 47
    levels 107–8, 120
    shortage of 88
    and visualisation 112
Energy Dial 107–8
enthusiasm 153
environment 178
exercise 103, 105, 119, 151
    and Bodymind Network 24, 29
experience 178

Fast Track Communication System
        24–30, 35, 43
fear 85, 134, 135, 153
food 119, 151
Ford, Henry 99
forgiveness 80, 151, 174, 178
    and emotional release 165–8
    and inner peace 47
    and relationships 72, 73
    of self 74, 75, 76–8

giving and receiving 170, 174, 178
goals 178
    achievement of 128–47
    and Bodymind Directions 145–6
    choice of 125–8
    defined 124
    and Inner Wisdom 125–7
    keeping commitment to 143
    in life 123–47
Goethe, Johann Wolfgang von 133
gratitude 170–2, 174, 178
greed 152–3
guidance 143
guilt 75, 78, 85, 152–3, 168
    and forgiveness 165–8
'gut feelings' 11

happiness 1, 2, 7
    in adversity 2–3

and Body Mind Directions 17, 21–2,
        43, 177
    as decision 177
    defined 8
    in the here and now 7, 119, 123
    and inner peace 47–8, 50
    and Inner Wisdom 42
    maximisation 57–9, 80
    and self-acceptance 85
    and smiling 51
    and thoughts 87–103
    and visualisation 37–42
happiness path 91–2, 93, 103, 109
hatred 152–3
healing
    and meditation 155
    processes 9, 60, 61
health 151
    and body image 103
    and Bodymind Directions 24, 29, 43,
        86, 117–19, 177
    and breathing 110
    commitment to 178
    and goal achievement 146
    and Higher Level Communication
        System 32
    and Inner Wisdom 42
    issues 142
    and positive thoughts 88–9
    and visualisation 112
heart rate 11
Higher Level Communication System
        30–6, 43
hugging 168–70, 174
hurt 161

images 34–5
imagination 31
immune system 50, 61
Incentive Card 143
inner child 161–5, 174
'inner critic' 87
inner life 86
inner peace see peace, inner
inner powers see powers, inner
inner self 8, 9, 12
    contact with 30, 33–6
    resources 35–6
    see also Inner Wisdom
Inner Voice 7–9
Inner Wisdom 2, 7, 8, 9
    and Bodymind Directions 15
    and desired changes 9, 86
    energising power of 39
    and goals in life 124–7
    guidance by 102, 177
    and healing process 42
    and Higher Level Communication
        System 32–6

and question and answer system 24,
    29, 30
and visualisation 135
innocence 162
inspiration from others 143

jealousy 152
joy 57, 155
'Just Being' 59–63

law of attraction 22
learning experiences 159, 178
leisure activities 7, 119, 124, 142
    commitment to 178
    and goal achievement 146
letting go 64, 65, 67–8, 160, 161, 178
    and forgiveness 75, 166
    of thoughts 17, 90, 92, 94–8
life 102, 123
listening skills 70–1, 80, 92–4, 162
love 2, 153–5
    and body image 104
    and Bodymind Directions 17, 22
    definitive characteristics 152
    and full life 149–79
    and happy moments 58, 59
    and hugging 168–70
    and ideal life 151, 174
    nurturing of 161–3, 174
    and thought patterns 94
loving kindness
    and inner child 165
    in listening 71
    and meditation 62, 66, 68, 160
    and relationships 73, 74
'loving kindness' meditation 60
'Loving Meditation' 155–61, 174

Maharishi Mahesh Yogi 59
mantra meditation 59, 68–70
martial arts 47
meditation 59–70
    and attitude 64
    benefits of 61
    and breath awareness 63, 65–8, 169
    and 'Breathe and Smile' mantra 52,
        59
    and energy 156–7
    and exercise 105
    for inner peace 65–8, 70
    and love 155–61
    and self-discovery 61
    and Shake Dance 107
mind
    focus for 64
    nature of 64–5
    power in 89–91, 98–101
    subconscious 101
'mindfulness' 59–60

mission statement 128–9, 130, 135,
    143
moment, present 51, 52, 80, 123, 151
moods see emotions
muscle relaxation 110

nervous system 106
Nhich Nhat Hanh 72

oxygen 109, 110

pain
    and Bodymind Directions 86, 117–19
    and Bodymind Network 11
    and endorphins 50
peace 1, 2, 35
    and Higher Level Communication
        System 31
    inner 45–81, 178
        and Bodymind Directions 17, 21,
            78–80
        and goal achievement 146
        maximisation of 57–9, 80
        and meditation 61, 62, 64, 70
        and relationships 71–3
        sharing with others 70–1
        and 'smile bath' 56
        and walking 53
    and 'Loving Meditation' 155, 156, 160
    and present moment 51, 52
    and questioning 26
    and visualisation 37–41, 41, 138
perfectionism 152
Pert, Dr 11
Pilates 104–5
pleasure 17, 57, 58
'Power in your Mind' 89–91
powers
    inner 2, 5–43
        and goal achievement 129–33
        and meditiation 61
        unleashing 42
        and visualisation 37–41
    of thought 88, 89–91, 119
praise 85, 102
present moment 51, 52, 119, 169,
    170, 178
purpose in life 123

question and answer system 12, 24,
    26–30, 29
    examples of questions 29
    and goals in life 124
    and Higher Level Communication
        System 32
    and loving 154–5
    signals for 'yes' and 'no' 24–9
    variations in answers 29–30, 32
quietening session 18–19

relationships 2, 142
    commitment to 178
    constructive 80
    and goal achievement 146
    healing 73–4
    and inner peace 47
    and meditation 62, 161
relaxation
    and energy 156–7
    exercises 155
    and Higher Level Communication
        System 31, 32–6
    and meditation 60
    and visualisation 36, 37, 38–9
'relaxation response' 50
religion 59
resentment 74, 78, 151, 152–3, 159
    and forgiveness 165
retribution 22
risks 133, 134

self 83–120
    and Bodymind Directions 116–20
    and loving 154
    younger 161
self-acceptance 7
self-awareness 62
self-esteem 85, 103
    and goal attainment 123, 146
    and visualisation 112, 116, 120
self-love 156
self-worth 103–4
selfishness 152
senses 62
sensitivity 162
setbacks 178
Shake Dance 106–7
situations
    challenging 86
    interpretation of 91–2
sleep and rest 103, 107, 108, 151
'smile bath' 56, 80
smiling 171
    and goal achievement 132
    and happiness 50, 51–6
    and inner peace 47–8
    and Start-up Body Mind Directions 17
'Smiling Mantra' see 'Breathe and
        Smile' Mantra
speech patterns 92–4
spirituality 32, 43
    and Bodymind Directions 23, 177
    commitment to 178
    experience of 59, 156, 157, 160
    and goal achievement 146
Start-up Bodymind Directions 16–18,
        20, 21, 24

and experiences 16–17
and questions 24, 25–6
'STOP! technique' 99–100, 102
strength, inner 47
'stress response' 109
stress-relief 171
success 128–33, 134, 142, 178
    and Bodymind Directions 177

tai chi 105
telephone 54
tension 87
therapy see healing; health
thoughts
    and awareness-raising 94–6
    and body cell structure 88
    control of 86, 89–91
    effect on self 85–6
    happy 87
    in meditation 67–8
    nature of 64–5
    negative 87–9, 152–3, 162
        challenged 98–9
        defined 92–4
        eliminated 99–100
        letting go of 94–8
    positive 96–7, 100–2, 151, 171
    power of 88, 99–100
time and time management 8, 10, 12,
        53
'Total Fulfilment' visualisation 135
Transcendental Meditation 59
Tuning-in 18–21, 78–9
    and goal achievement 145
    and questions 24, 25

understanding 71–3, 80, 151, 153,
        161

vanity 152–3
visualisation 2, 36–7, 111–16, 120
    and Bodymind Network 112
    with inner child 163–5
    'Total Fulfilment' 135–47
Voice, Inner see Inner Voice

walking 53
water exercise 105
Wisdom,Inner see Inner Wisdom
work 142, 148, 178
worry see anxiety

'yes' and 'no' signals 24–5, 26–30
yoga 104–5

THE FIVE FEEL GOOD FACTORS
AUDIOTAPE

Order Jan Sadler's inspirational audiotape on which Jan's relaxing voice leads you through the beautiful 'Ideal You' and 'The Key to True Happiness' visualisations.

ORDER FORM

Name...

Adress ....

....

....

....

.... Post Code...............

Please send me .... copies of the 'Ideal You' Audiotape at £9.00 per tape, including post and packing.

I enclose my cheque for £..........

Please make cheques payable to Jan Sadler and send to:

Creative Health, 1 Penoweth, Mylor Bridge, Falmouth TR11 5NQ.

Also look at Jan Sadler's website: www.painsupport.co.uk